HALF-DEAD

HALF-DEAD

...Means You're Still Half Alive

BYRON JOYCE

AVVENTURA PRESS

Eynon, PA

Photos by Vicki Cronis

Cover and interior design by Lee Sebastiani, Avventura Press

Copyright ° 2008 by Byron Joyce. All rights reserved.

Library of Congress Control Number: 2008929877

ISBN-13: 978-0-9761553-3-1
Published by
Avventura Press
133 Handley St.
Eynon PA 18403-1305
570-876-5817
www.avventurapress.com

2nd printing August 2008

Printed in the United States of America

DEDICATION

This book is dedicated to the loving memory of Mrs. Rosa Hines who had so much love and support for me she made it difficult to fail. Also to my man Ronald Caldwell—wish you was here, big guy—and Derrius "Woo Woo" Walton. R.I.P.

ACKNOWLEDGEMENTS

This project is an extension of my soul. I've worked long and hard to complete this book and it could not have been done without the love, encouragement, and support of those around me.

First of all, I would like to give thanks to God, who is the orchestra leader of this symphony that has become my life. The grace and the mercies He showed toward me were more than I deserve.

I would also say a special thanks to my mother who worked so hard to keep us in line and worked hard every day to try and keep the lights burning and food on the table. Thanks to my father who finally got himself together in time to be an inspiration in my recovery. To my wife and children for loaning me out for the time it took to complete this venture.

To Rev. Jake Manley and the Showers of Blessings staff that saw me through my addiction. To Mrs. Isabelle Mitchell for showing special love and favor toward me. Big ups to my special sons Russell and Keon for following instruction and becoming real men. Much love to Tawanna "Sugar" Branch who started it all and Shalyse who kept pressure on me not to quit. Thanks for my grand baby Tionni, much love Tee Tee and T.J.

To all my adopted children (too many to name) that I love very much. A very special thanks to my brother from another mother. Mike for his support and motivation that wouldn't let this project die. A special shout out to Vicky and Denise my partners in crime—without you guys this wouldn't be possible. Last but not least thanks to Lee for a chance to brighten people's lives. *God bless you all.*

FOREWORD

When I first met Byron he was scary. His street name was "Jaws." *Perfect*, I thought. *It suits him.* He looked as mean as a shark! He'd developed that reputation on the street. "Jaws" was known for being big.... Tough....And flat crazy!

I met him at an inner city church service. I was the only white guy in the pew.

When we were introduced, he looked at this tall, skinny white guy, like, "He's gotta be five-oh...or a reporter!!

Well, at least I wasn't a cop. And I really didn't want a story. I had come to a service at this predominately black church to see first-hand a program that was helping to change lives.

I saw something in Byron when we met that was hard to pinpoint, but he had a gift of communicating in a unique way. On the street or in the pulpit.

We didn't say *boo* to each other months after we met at the church. I got to know some other guys in the program, but not him.

But I did see how Byron looked at guys who were dealing or using—not as addicts or dealers or criminals. He looked at them the same way we all want to be viewed, as someone with value, purpose and potential yet to be realized.

What's unique about Byron then and now is that he points to a relationship with God as the only hope...the only help. He doesn't point to Byron, to the church, or to any program. He won't point to this book, either.

But you might!

Oh, yeah.....After all these years, I still occasionally call my best friend, "Jaws." It wasn't until almost a year after I met Byron that I found out he was given the street name "Jaws" not because of his viciousness, but because...he talked too much.

His "jaws" never stopped flappin'!

Television News Anchor Mike Lewis

Introduction

I spent my early teenage and adult life in a place called Berkley. This isn't Berkeley, California, with the ritzy schools and spoiled rich kids that you always hear about. The children in this community are predominately underprivileged and for most going to school isn't really a priority. What *is* important is where their next meal is coming from and how they're going to get it.

This isn't the Berkeley where you see movie crews on the local corners. In this Berkley if there *are* cameras, they're usually accompanied by police sirens and the cameramen belong to a news team. There are thousands of stories in this Berkley. The stars of these miniseries all have the same role. Their role is a person trying to survive in a desperate situation. Their award is just to be living and not locked up the next day. The words *Lights! Camera! Action!* have been replaced with *Where is the action?*

Berkley is a neighborhood just a stone's throw from downtown Norfolk, Virginia. General MacArthur's mother lived in Berkley back in the day. There's still a memorial testifying to that historical fact. A city within a city as it's commonly referred to, Berkley once had everything—movie theater, funeral homes, its own ambulance service. You name it; the predominately white population of Berkley had it. Berkley was a proud community.

By the time I moved to Berkley its great history was over. Its Caucasian residents had slowly disappeared. The buildings were old, and the morals of the people living there were declining. Drugs and alcohol had become a major destructive force in the community. My friends and I weren't the only reason, but we were a big part of Berkley's decline.

This is Berkley East during the mid-seventies through the early nineties. Berkley was going through a major transformation and I witnessed at first hand the drastic changes. Businesses were closing, middle class citizens were scrambling to get out of the community and the houses were being filled with welfare recipients and Section Eight clients. Mothers were the bread winners of the household, and were doing their best to keep their families afloat alone. All of these things together combined to create a toxic atmosphere to grow up in.

After being introduced to these conditions my life drastically changed. I auditioned for and was awarded a leading role in this saga. I became a high school dropout and eventually a strung-out crackhead. Berkley presented great obstacles for me that very well could have caused me to throw in the towel, but I persevered. Selfish people would have kept this very personal story to themselves, but I chose to share it that you might also consider triumph instead of defeat.

This story really begins when I was a teenager. My mom and dad had split up and it weighed heavily on me. Byron Joyce was making decisions according to what he believed. Trying to become a man by watching his uninformed friends, who were also trying to make their passage to manhood. We had no real example of what a man was so we winged it. The blind leading the blind, you could say.

Statistics say this story should be an obituary, but it's not. It *is* the testimony of a man who shouldn't have lived to be twenty-five. A bright young man whose brightness only made his surroundings seem darker. I am the poster child for nature versus nurture, not only in my life, but also the lives of the young people whom I've touched. The children that God has graciously given to me shouldn't have been born, and the other children I've helped to turn around should not have had the chance to make my acquaintance. I could have been just another black youth, a victim of drugs and violence, who died in the poverty and ignorance of another ghetto. Yet I was granted mercy to survive and be able to tell this story of my pain, despair, and eventual ultimate triumph.

ONE

I was born in Norfolk Community Hospital, a brand-new resident of Tidewater Park. Tidewater Park was a low-income housing project in Norfolk, Virginia where all of the buildings looked the same and most of the residents shared the same sad testimony—"doom, despair, and agony on me." The Park, as it was commonly called, featured alcoholism on parade. Cocaine and heroin weren't seen on the streets (at least I never really saw it) but evidence of alcohol use was on display on every corner. Bushes cluttered with empty bottles were a part of the landscape. Houses called "shot houses" or "nip joints" were on every block. The Virginia Alcoholic Beverage Control "ABC" store wasn't far from our community in the downtown plaza.

These shot houses produced characters like Joe Beast, who always carried a switchblade and had no problem using it. Mr. "No Talk" Ricks was another member of this fraternity. He had a terrible stuttering problem, which only got worse once he started drinking. It wasn't uncommon at all to see someone stumble until they fell because of alcohol. Staggering drunks were a common sight in this part of Norfolk. You'd meet these types of characters in The Park on a daily basis.

My parents were Alvin and Mary Joyce, a couple of North Carolinians who had settled in the neighborhood to try to raise a family. I was number eight of ten children born to this union. At the beginning of their marriage, my mother was a homemaker who doubled as a waitress. She was working at Giant Open Air Market on Campostella Road in Norfolk. For me, the best part of her job was that she would bring stuff home after work. She'd cross the doorstep with caramel popcorn balls, pizza, and doughnuts, just to name a few. She was a sweet woman who didn't hesitate to give her children a whipping when she thought they needed it, but still she was a hard working provider. If she had one fault it was choosing Alvin Joyce to be the father of her children.

On the other hand, my father Alvin was a habitual drinker and was well known at the shot houses. During my childhood I can't remember him ever being sober. "A.J.," as we referred to him, was a fun loving, drunken hell-raiser. He would always come home looking for a fight. Little things like the lights in the house would send him on a rampage. If the lights were on, he'd want them off. If they were off, he'd prefer them on. He'd say something like "Why all the lights out in here? Y'all act like you blind. Cut some damn lights on!" He'd just seem to bring drama along whenever he showed up. He was notorious for losing his keys and even his car a time or two. Legend has it that once in a drunken stupor, he ran through a gas station tearing up the gas pumps.

My mother was patient with his foolishness. I've seen pictures of my mother when she was young. She was so fine. Looking back, it's hard to imagine a beautiful woman like my mom staying with a pot-bellied drunk so long. But that would soon change.

After suffering many years of his alcohol abuse, diminishing finances, and even allegations of womanizing, my mother decided to try to make it on her own. She had put together a plan and executed it at the proper time. By then, she had gotten some schooling and used it to land a job at the community mental health agency with the City of Norfolk. The job was a blessing for her and our family, but without the little bit of money my father brought home as a truck driver, life would still be difficult financially. Nonetheless, she was fed up and ready to make a change.

The last night that I can remember us being together as a family was in September, 1974. My father had entered the house drunk as usual. After a few minutes of my father's meddling an argument began between my mother and father. This time the argument between my parents ended with violence. My mother grabbed a pool stick from our little ragged pool table and broke the pool stick on my father. My younger brothers and I were in bed but we heard the commotion.

"Why you hit me with the stick, Teen?" my father said. (Christine was her name, but he called her "Teen" for short)

"Why you hit me with the stick?"

I never had known my mother to be violent. The only people I had ever seen her hit was us, her children. Guess she was fed up and released all those years of frustration in one big swing of that pool stick. Don't recall where he was hit but the blow was hard enough to break the stick.

That night was the longest night of my life. Most of the night was spent peeking out into the hallway and hoping that my father wouldn't seek revenge. Our room was located between my mother and father's' bedrooms. They were sleeping in separate rooms at the time. I stayed awake until I couldn't hold my eyes open anymore. I woke up the next morning and my mother was okay. We got dressed and went to school as usual.

By morning my mother's plan was underway. She had made arrangements to rent a house over in Berkley. She did all this in secrecy. The day started like a typical day. My father, recovering from his pool cue wounds, went to work and we went to school. After school, a Cadillac parked outside of my school at Ruffner Junior High was our taxi to a new world and a new existence. Some of my mother's friends picked up my brother Dwayne (Doo Wop) and me from school. The car belonged to the Hodges family, our soon to be next-door neighbors.

The car drove an unusual route. The trip got really frightening when we crossed the Berkley Bridge. I can still hear the sound of the tires as they rolled over the grids of the drawbridge. My heart was in my throat as we descended down the slope of the bridge and entered Berkley. Every turn increased my heart rate and my desire for Tidewater Park and my daddy. My eyes were glued to the window as we passed through the maze of streets that led to our new home.

Old wooden houses lined the streets of Berkley. It was like a trip to the country. The car seemed to travel in slow motion as we drove through this mystical part of Norfolk. The only thing I knew about Berkley was that there was a swimming pool there, but it wasn't a safe place to go. I had heard the horror stories about kids from "The Park" who tried to visit that pool only to be run back across the bridge by the hoodlum children of Berkley.

The trip to my new home was as frightful as the episode that took place the night before at my old place. The car finally came to a stop at 1002 South Main Street, a shabby looking old white house trimmed in green. The huge trees around the house gave it the spookiest feeling. The big roots of the trees grew on the surface of the ground. I knew the life that I had before was over. How my heart longed for Tidewater Park!

Up to this point life had been okay. My family was not as tight as I would like it to be, but it would do. I was an decent student and striving to be a world changer but now, at this place, at this time, the only thing I wanted to change was my address. I was afraid. I was a young teenage boy caught up in grown folks' bad decisions and there was nothing I could do about it. Life is anything but fair. You live, go through hell, then you die. That was my feeling about life overall. No matter your race, creed or color, trouble is no respect of person. "Into each life some rain must fall." I don't know where that quote came from but it's so right it ought to be in the Bible. If you live you are going to run into some rain and if you haven't, you keep living and it's on the way. By now I was receiving buckets. Even when you don't look for it, rain or trouble sort of has a way of finding you.

Questions danced in my head. Where was I? What would I do about school? Most of all, where was my daddy? Somehow I looked for him to deliver me. Even though he was always drunk, and never read me a bedtime story, or came to any of my games in football or basketball, I still wanted him, now more than ever. I knew that he wasn't going to be my deliverance, but I hoped he would show up. I still had much love for him, because after all, he was still my dad and I missed him.

After being here for a while, I recognize it's not the hand that you're dealt, it's how you play the cards. Even though I usually wore my poker face, I was not happy with the dealer. The hand I was dealt would have a big influence on the events that would shape and mold me. The people, places, and things in my cards are directly responsible for some of the horror I've been through, and the person I turned out to be.

A great part of my recovery has come from recalling where and when the roller coaster ride started. Looking back can help you to move forward. No ordeal just happens. There is normally slow but steady progression that leads to hardship. It's like the erosion of the coastline. The beach doesn't disappear in one great wave, but the constant pounding of the surf however slight eventually causes a change. You look up one day and the coastline is gone.

Most times we want to believe that trouble just all of a sudden happens, but if you check your situation closely you will find patterns that lead you to your place of hardship. Trouble is no respecter of person. Without warning, you look up one day and life as you knew it is gone. That bank account just didn't pop up empty. That relationship showed signs of collapse before now. Your drug habit may have started long before you took that first hit of any drug. That gambling habit didn't all of a sudden just happen. Recognizing where my process started has been a great tool to help untangle the mess that had become my life.

Childhood is a great place to start looking for beginnings of trouble. A child is born with a brain and not a mind. The mind is developed from the things that happen around us. Every bad habit we have we learned from somewhere. Some of the circumstances we have lived through have served as good teachers and triggers of bad decisions and bad behaviors. Search your past; it may be a great help to propel your future.

TWO

The transition from Tidewater Park to Berkley brought much trial and tribulation. I was looking for a place to fit in, in a place where I really didn't want be. It wasn't long before I started to meet the cast of characters who would play a major role in my development as a person. They weren't bad people, but like me, they all had issues stemming from the mistakes their parents had made as well as their environment. I adopted their behaviors and created a destructive person that I didn't really recognize. I started to develop my crackhead personality.

My first, combative encounter came after I was enrolled at Lake Taylor Junior High School in 1974. I was riding the old TRT bus home from school (they were the school buses back then). The trip was about twenty minutes each way on these old buses. And if that wasn't bad enough, Tony Barksdale, a kid from the neighborhood, decided he wanted to throw paper at me. I used to sit in the exit doorway in the back of the bus. I chose to sit there because I didn't want to bother anyone and most of all I didn't want anyone to bother me. Tony kept pestering me until I sprang from the exit stairs of the bus to confront him. With the frustration of being at a strange school, my family's being separated, and riding without a seat, Tony's paper game was as much as I could stand. A kid named

Darryl Jefferson stepped in between me and Tony. As he intervened in the disturbance, in a whisper he reminded me that Tony was the cousin of Calvin Barksdale. Tony stood about five-feet-two and manageable, but Calvin was what seemed at the time to be six-one and all muscle. He was someone you really didn't want to have problems with, so after a couple of seconds of stares I declined to take any further action. I acted as if I wanted to, but Darryl's warning was good enough for me to redirect my desire.

I was sentenced to Lake Taylor Junior High School for my educational needs. At Lake Taylor I was placed in modified classes, which were set up for students who weren't cutting it in regular classes. They were packed with troubled kids, kids that I wouldn't want my children hooked up with. I never really got to know people in class because I stayed to myself, but I did observe them. I didn't consider myself a modified student. At Ruffner I was a pretty good student, but after being in class with my new associates, slowly my behavior began to match my classmates'.

School was no longer important, adults had started losing my respect, and my grades plummeted. I was always in trouble in one form or another. Calvin "Kung Fu" Fonville was a very strange guy in my English class. He used to walk around yelling "Boom! Pop! Train! I shoot the game! I shoot the moon!" As ridiculous as I thought that sounded, I decided to go try it myself. I walked into the band classroom (and I wasn't even a student in that class)—"Boom! Pop! Train! Boom! Pop! Train!"

The Band teacher was not amused by my antics. He called for me and I took off running. To my surprise the teacher gave chase after me. When I say chased I mean *chased*. The guy must have had some troubles at home or something because he ran after me like I was something to eat and he was hungry. The pursuit went on for about ten minutes. I ran from hall to hall; the teacher pursued. I ran outside the building; the man never stopped. Sharp speedy cuts around corners by me could not persuade him to stop coming after me. He was possessed, a man on a mission and like Dudley Do-Right, he was determined to get his man. The brisk jog for freedom ended when I ran into Mr. Stone, the gym teacher. Mr. Stone was a caveman-type guy. He was strong and muscular, with a thick scruffy beard, and he ran around the track at school every day for exercise. I figured it might be smarter to submit to him than try to outrun him.

I began to fail classes on a regular basis. During the next four semesters, if I passed *any* classes it was a miracle. My fear of my mother was starting to diminish and I was on a roller coaster ride, high speed, for jails, institutions or death.

I started to get braver and began to take more chances. I didn't expect anything bad would happen if I ventured out of my normal circle, but I knew it was possible. One night I decided to visit a young lady who had moved from "The Park" to Berkley. She and her family had a place in Bell Diamond Manor about six blocks from my house on South Main Street. I had walked up to this area before, but it was during the day. This was slightly after dark and I thought it would be okay. As I walked up Liberty Street I noticed a group of guys walking in my direction. I continued to walk, (slightly shaken but not stirred) towards the group. Soon I was surrounded by this mob of guys looking for something fun to do. I just happened to be that fun.

Steve "Brute" Atkins, a man so crazy that he would dress in full football gear, helmet, shoulder pads—the whole nine yards—just to play touch football, and Barry Mullen, who had to be the biggest thirteen or fourteen-year old kid you've ever seen in your life. Nathaniel "Magnificent" Walton, Amos "Mikey" Cherry, the Turner Boys, David "Jumpshot" Judice were just a few of the faces in this crowd. The mob consisted of at least twenty-five young aggressive African American males. They introduced themselves with "What you doing down here?"

They didn't wait to hear my answer. I was beaten, dragged, and punched, not really violent blows but humiliating all the same. Karate movies were big in those days, so they held me while they practiced their karate kicks on me. After about ten minutes or so, my captors released me. I was left in the street with one shoe on and one shoe off. They used my other shoe to pelt me about the head. I'll never forget sitting humiliated on the curb and strapping on that red Pro Ked sneaker.

The walk home was long and thoughtful. I was battered and bruised but not broken. I thought to myself, *I can't go home like this. How am I going to face myself in the morning? What guarantee do I have that this won't happen again?* A wise man once told me, "If there is no consequence, there can be no change." Somebody had to be held responsible for this whipping and who better to enforce it than me? I was angry as hell anyway. A new neighborhood I didn't want, grades shot, daddy gone. What did I have to lose? I turned about face, dried my tears and went searching for the challenge of my life.

I walked through Bell Diamond Manor toward a dimly lit park. Faint voices got louder as I drew closer to where the mob had gathered. I walked up, and there was a buzz among the mob when they noticed me. Somebody in the crowd yelled, "Oh, he want some more!"

My answer to that foolish notion was swift. "Not like that!" I exclaimed, and quickly I followed with "But I *will* fight one of you, one on one."

I must have lost my mind. Maybe the beating I had received had done more damage than I thought. It wasn't like I was this great fighter in the first place. I mean I had won my fair share of boyhood fights but I had lost a few also. Nevertheless it was out there now and I couldn't take it back. The crowd got excited. They let me pick the guy I wanted to fight. Looking at the crowd, my choices ranged from Little Dave to Big Barry Mullen and every size in between. I chose right down the middle. I figured if I chose somebody about my size the natives wouldn't become restless and they'd let it be a fair fight. I was almost right.

My victim was Toby Etheridge. Toby and I squared off and immediately I began to take my anger out on him. I had one hand cuffed in Toby's collar and the other hand I used to pound him. He would swing; I would duck most of his shots and continue to connect with mine. Some in the crowd were cheering me on but that didn't last. Before I knew it I was grabbed from behind and then punched in the face by Mikey Cherry while being held by someone else. I absorbed the blows and asked, "Can we finish what we started?"

Immediately, Toby and I resumed our fight. I had grabbed hold of his shirt collar and swung him around, hitting him with occasional punches, and just like before I was interrupted by Mikey and his partners. Barry Mullen stepped in. When I saw him make his move toward me I thought, *Oh well, life is over.* He threw his arm around me and said, "Go home, man. You can't win."

Little did he know I already felt like I gained a victory. I got my chance to hit someone and I was still alive. What was I thinking? What I chose to do in this situation wasn't very smart, but I was glad I did it. Now I could go home in peace. Black-eyed and a little bruised, but still I felt better than I did after the first whipping. I guess this was my initiation into the Berkley family of misfits.

If you really want to know the situation you're in, check the people you're involved with. The old adage "association brings on assimilation" is as true as gospel itself. Normally, you are what your friends and associates are. No matter how strong you think you are, if you hang in certain places you will soon succumb to the behaviors of those around you.

In the movie Trading Places, *two Wall Street traders make a bet, one believing that change of scenery and circumstance would change a street-wise bum's behavior, the other trader opposing that belief. The bum was taken off the street, placed in the new environment and converted into a Wall Street stock tycoon. Just like the trader in the movie, I believe that you are a product of the place you are raised and the situation surrounding your life.*

The Gaderene, a man in the Bible, was known to live amongst the tombs. Tombs are where they bury dead people. There is no way that his behavior was going to be anything greater than dead. He had no clue how to live, how to act or how to solve problems because the place where he dwelled was full of dead people. The only thing he really wanted to do was be dead like those who surrounded him. At one point in the story the young man starts to cut himself with stones.

For those of you with cell phones, check the people whose numbers you have saved in your contact list. You probably will notice that the majority of the contacts you have are of people in the same or similar situation as you. There is no way those people are going to be able to uplift you. Delete those from your contact list that will hold you back from your goals. If there are no positive numbers in your phone just throw the whole phone away.

The message here is, if you are trying to make changes in your life the first change has to be the people you associate with and the environments you are accustom to spending your time in.

THREE

Four years had passed since my mother moved us from "The Park." Berkley life was a whole lot different from living in Tidewater Park. There were so many places to go and people to see. I began to experience a whole new world in Berkley. I was starting to become known in the neighborhood.. Berkley had its own fire station, ambulance service, and two or three funeral homes. One of the funeral homes, called the Metropolitan, featured Mr. Bazemore, who was a scary figure to say the least. Mr. Bazemore also doubled as the ambulance driver. His alleged claim to fame was that he once turned over a police car. His King Kongish look made this legend easy to believe. (Incidentally my thoughts at the time were, *if I ever need an ambulance or a funeral home please don't call Metropolitan.* I just couldn't stand the thought of being picked up by Mr. Bazemore.) Nevertheless the sights and sounds of Berkley were beginning to feel like home.

Stores lined Liberty Street and there were small nightclubs all over the place, like Sparrows, Black Cats Lounge, George Perkins, and Moore's Lounge. As I ventured around, it seemed exciting, so different from the plain brick apartments in Tidewater Park, which were all stuck together and looked the same. Berkley had alleys and churches and pool halls. One was located at the corner of Berkley Avenue and State Street. This pool hall became one of the major classrooms in the mis-education of Byron Joyce.

I never really became a good student in school again; I did just enough to get by. I had to repeat the eighth grade and school wasn't a priority. By the time I was a senior I knew just about everybody. I even had a nickname. *Jabba Jaws.* Two innocent children who thought I looked like the cartoon character gave me that name. I marketed the name to emphasize my golden-tongued gift of gab. The mob that had attacked me in my Berkley initiation became my friends and I strove to keep their approval. I did what they did. We formed a group or gang called the Airplanes. We shared a similar characteristic—almost all of us had no father in our home and our mothers were managing the household. We had limited contact with our fathers so at best we learned how to be men through trial and error. We were fifteen-year-old teenagers teaching each other to be men.

The Airplanes affiliation was at first mostly sports related. I grew up with some real athletes. The Airplanes were AAU boxers, baseball, football, and basketball players. With the exception of myself and a few others, these guys had at least Division I potential. We developed teams and coached ourselves; we competed against the adults of the community.

One of the most memorable events was the annual Turkey Bowl game. We played against other teams from local neighborhoods. One year, we played against players who were legends of our neighborhood like Donald "Coal Jack" Foreman and Donnie "Icky Boo" Mann. These guys were awesome athletes and were well-respected and feared in the community. This game was a huge spectacle in Berkley. Crowds from all the local communities would come to see it. Every year just like the famous Harlem Globetrotters, the Airplanes would emerge victorious. But the talents we had slowly turned toward petty crimes and violence by our early twenties. Stealing spoked hubcaps off cars, ripping off convenience stores for ham and cheese, Oreos, and candy became our M.O. We were well known but not really accepted at social events. But we still managed to find the parties and crash them. We'd always wind up at the table were the food was. More often than not, when the food was gone, so were we.

One night at a party in Regina Perkin's backyard Darryl Jefferson and I were talking when we noticed a guy dancing with a fine girl. We had a saying, "The girl was so fine that I'd drink her bath water," and for this girl we would drink gallons. As she danced I fantasized about having the chance to be with her. I cut in on the dance, and the guy cut me right back. *Wow*, I thought, *that was inconsiderate*, so I went on to cut in on the dance again. He immediately cut me back. I went and got my friend and fellow Airplane Darryl and told him what had just transpired. Darryl and I put together a plan. I tapped the guy on his shoulder on one side as Darryl proceeded to cut in from the other side. The fellow finally started to show his frustration and replaced Darryl as the girl's partner quickly and gave him an evil look. Darryl then tapped him on the shoulder, and I jumped in to dance with his date again. This time he pushed me. When I turned he punched me in my face. *This man has to be crazy*, I thought. I retaliated with two blows, knocking him to the ground. As Darryl and I had our way with this guy, the mauling was broken up and the party resumed.

Other members of our crew started to arrive. By now the Airplanes were in full force. At least fifteen of us had shown up by now. After maybe thirty minutes the Planes had gathered around and I began to tell the story of the earlier fiasco. While I was telling the story somebody stepped through the crowd and hit me in the head with an object. I figured it was the same guy back for revenge but I wasn't sure. This time when I went to retaliate I felt something on my face and brushed it away. That something turned out to be a stream of blood left by the sneak attack. I retreated, hit the ground and rolled through the yard until I made it to the street. Nursing my wound I looked back in the yard and it looked like the Wild West. Bikes and trashcans were flying. People were running and screaming. Punches were being thrown; it was chaos. I hustled back to the yard with a trashcan to inflict some pain of my own.

Before long the fight escalated into a chase down Campostella Road. I'll never know if the guys we caught were even the enemy, but they received a terrible whipping for being in the path of the Airplanes' fury. I still can see Steve Atkins jumping off the edge of a ditch onto one young fellow's face and Mikey Cherry punching another. I had been the victim of Mikey's punches before, so I knew first-hand the agony my man was going through. Five or six others including myself joined in on the blows. The guys in the ditch were screaming for help. Cars lined the street blowing their horns but the beating didn't stop until the cries for help did. I remember walking back to the party with my face bloody like a pro wrestler, wearing my war wounds proudly.

We started to adopt each other as brothers. Even though the Airplanes were one big dysfunctional family, we had subdivisions. My brothers included Barry Mullen. Being his brother was a no-brainer; he was the biggest and most respected in the group. We used to say that Barry could hit a wet tree and shake every drop of water from it with one blow. My other brother was Nathanel "Magnificent" Walton. Some of the worst events in my life involved these two fellows. One night Magnificent was high on a chemical. He was under the impression that his car was running out of gas. With a few of us in his car, he sped down the interstate highway trying to find a gas station. His mad dash came to a halt when he attempted to exit the interstate. His speed was too high to make the turn. We were headed straight for a cement pillar holding up the overpass. By the grace of God the car turned just in time. When the tires on the passenger side hit the curb the car nearly flipped. Heads hit the roof of the car; luckily no one was seriously injured. Another brush with death for me and my personal angel, whom I'd keep ever so busy.

Walt was also my accomplice in a book heist at our high school during my senior year. It all started when I noticed a young man leaving the bookroom with a book. The bookroom was supposed to be closed and the lights were out. I knew something was suspicious.

At this time students had to buy their textbooks. I informed the young man that if he didn't get me my books too there was going to be a problem. He turned around and went back in the bookroom, put his book back and told me to do my own dirty work.

Hustling was in my blood and this was a chance not only to get the books I needed, but also to spark my budding entrepreneurial spirit. I stole about ten books and put the word out that I had books for sale. The books sold like hotcakes. I just knew this could be bigger, so after school, Walt and I returned to the bookroom and stole every book we could carry. My locker was just down the hallway. We filled the locker with English and social studies books. The next school day Jabba's book company was on and popping. I sold books cheaper than the school did so sales came easy. (This sales practice I would continue in future entrepreneurship adventures.) They sold so fast that at lunchtime I had to make another hit. During lunch while the halls were nice and busy, I made my move again. I used a paper clip to open the door of the bookroom, grabbed an armful of the day's best-sellers and hit the hallway with my bounty like a wolf with a mouth full of lamb.

While making my mad dash with my newly acquired fortune I was spotted by the janitor. He followed me toward the lockers, but because of the crowd, I had time to ditch the books in a girl's locker before he could get close to me. I continued down the hallway to my locker. Unknown to me another guy had just stolen some books too, and his locker was right next to mine. The janitor came up beside me and saw the books that were in the open locker. He put the blame on me. When he asked me what I was doing with those books, I said they weren't mine and went on to my class.

The janitor didn't have a name, he just had a description, but that was good enough. When you're a well-known troublemaker like I was at Lake Taylor High it wasn't hard to match the description to the person. I was summoned to the office. The walk seemed like the stroll to the death chamber. I knew I was in trouble—I just didn't know how deep. With every step I took, my mind was racing to construct an airtight lie that would get me over this drama. When I reached the office I was already convicted before I opened my mouth. Johnny Cochran couldn't get me out of this mess. After trying to no avail to convince the principal that the janitor was hallucinating, the police were called and my fate was sealed. Away to jail I went. Straight to jail—do not pass go, do not collect two-hundred bucks. Eighteen years old, locked up for the first time in my life and scared to death. I couldn't believe I was actually going to jail. Hey, I thought the worse that could happen was that I would get suspended, but I was in jail. This was not a game.

The next day I was brought into the courtroom. I was standing in front of a judge for the first time. I looked around and there he was—the janitor. He was in a suit and ready and willing to testify. The judge allowed me time to try and convince him that the janitor may have needed glasses but again my story fell on deaf ears. The judge found me guilty and sentenced me to fifteen days in the city jail. I felt railroaded. I was also scared out of my mind. When my fifteen-day sentence was read I broke out in hives from head to toe. I remember a Caucasian gentleman who was stumbling drunk screamed to the guard to get me help. He was so drunk he could hardly stand but he put forth a good effort to get me some assistance. Needless to say, the help never came. This was a bad day in my mixed-up life.

I didn't have any idea what was getting ready to happen to me. I had heard about rapes and even murders at in the jailhouse. Every one of the stories danced through my mind while I was waiting to be moved to a permanent cell. Fear and disappointment were my greatest emotions. Boy, did I want to go home. But this would be my new home at least for the next fifteen days.

My new address was 811 City Hall Avenue, a dormitory-type cell at Norfolk City Jail with over thirty other inmates. There were three urinals against the wall with no stalls around them. The toilets were right in front of an onlooking congregation of criminals. After all the stories I heard about jail, I hoped I wouldn't have to use these facilities to relieve myself for the next fifteen days. Of course I couldn't hold out that long and again I had to suffer another embarrassing moment. Sitting down on that stool for the first time was as humiliating as it comes. Here I was, taking a dump with an audience. It was like taking a prostate exam on national TV. This was a withdrawal from my self-esteem account. It was already marked "insufficient funds." People really didn't pay attention to you while you relieved yourself but you thought all eyes were on you.

My stay, although it seemed like forever, was only nine days. The day before I was scheduled to depart I mentioned to one of the inmates that I was leaving in the morning. He told me that the last day could be my worst day. He went on to say that some people wake up in a burning sheet on their last day. I spent the rest of the night trying to figure out how to escape a burning sheet. Thankfully I made it through the night. The next morning I was released and I ran all the way from 811 City Hall Avenue to my house in Berkley non-stop. The Berkley Bridge I'd been afraid to cross in a car was no challenge after leaving that hellhole. In reality I was running from one jail to another. Berkley had not changed. Neither was the old story that was waiting to greet me.

Looking back I wasn't born a bad person, I was just comfortable making bad decisions. That process of making those types of decisions would continue for a long time. The thing that we must remember is that some of those bad preferences can be so detrimental that they take years to recover from. A short journey can be very time consuming if we take the wrong directions. "There is a path that seemeth right to men but its end is destruction." I had no idea that the choices I was making could turn out so bad. But I've heard it said, "What can happen will happen."

Sometimes pride is a deterrent to making good decisions. Once you get on a roll for being stupid you act like stupid is the norm. Trying to prove to yourself and others that the decision you made wasn't a bad one, when all the while you know it was. If you have recognized that you are losing your grip on making sound decisions drop your pride, ask for help. The life you save may be your own. Trust me; other people are fully aware of your folly. The only person you are fooling is yourself.

I still bear a lot of the physical scars I acquired from making bad choices. I have scars on my face I received from a collision with an eighteen wheeler. A six inch scar on my cheek that runs from an inch short of my left eye to the tip of my smile. Keloid scars in my head that were gashes that once upon a time poured out real blood.

Under the influence of substances, people, and situations we can make bad choices. Just think of all the people who can't come back from the bad decisions they made. It's never too late to make a right *choice. Good decisions can even come on the heels of making a bad choice. On this journey of life there is always room for a u-turn. Stop, drop and roll. Stop where you are so that you don't let this situation take you deeper. Drop your pride; acknowledge your fault in the decision you have made. Get some help to minimize your damages. Most of all, roll on to the newness that a good decision will bring. Don't let miscues deter you. Your good fortune is out there and it will never come if you let failure keep you bound. Get up, brush yourself off and try something new. Start a roll of positive consequences by making one good decision at a time.*

FOUR

I can remember going to the store for Ms. Vivian when I was ten years old. I went home a many a day with a dirty nose and forehead from peeping through her dirty screen door. I would put my face to the door and ask "Ms. Vivian, do you need me to go to the store for you?" I knew that when I returned I would receive a few coins.

As I got a little older I would take people's groceries to their cars at the local market for tips. You name it, I did it. Collect and sell pop bottles, cut grass—any way to keep a couple of bucks in my pocket. So making the conversion to a street hustler became second nature.

My mother didn't have a lot of money. Eight of us were still living in the house with her. Just keeping a roof over our heads was a tough task. So expecting to get the latest designer jeans or the popular brand of sneakers was unrealistic. I wore whatever I could get my hands on. I often wore my brother's clothes including his active duty army uniforms. Nothing was off limits. I wore his entire dress uniform to school one day, stood on a chair in the lunchroom and posed in a salute for over ten minutes, much to the amusement of my classmates. I was embarrassed that these were the only clothes I had to wear, but I managed to turn the situation into a joke. If you are going to turn things around in your life you have to be willing to find something positive in a negative situation.

I used to go to the local thrift store and buy old suits and white shirts and ties. I had to make do with what I had. I've heard the saying, "When the world gives you lemons make lemonade." Having money was not one of my family's traits. I was always afraid they'd turn the lights off at our house or kick us out for not paying rent. Because of my family's financial situation and the absence of my so-called father, it became easy to give in to the temptations of quick money in the streets.

The streets were calling and they had my number on speed dial. Horace Duke's Pool Hall was a dusty, dimly lit place with five old pool tables. Another permanent fixture in the pool hall was Mr. Brown, a slow-shuffling old gentleman who was in charge of racking the balls and collecting the money. I had been expelled from school by now and the pool hall wasn't a good place to spend what would have been my senior year.

The poolroom had a curriculum of its own. I learned to shoot pool, mark cards, identify crooked dice and most important, how to get a few pair of my own. With nothing else to do but practice I got better at the craft of street hustling. I could pick up one pair of dice and switch to a crooked pair with a movement of my hand. Sometimes my skills were not up to par and I would occasionally expose myself by dropping more than I planned. I wasn't making a whole lot of money, but it was more money than I ever had in my life. Not only that, it felt good to be successful at something. The more I got the more I wanted. Still I felt this feeling of emptiness and inside I was searching for more.

One day while talking with "Big D" he informed me and Li'l Dave Judice that we could make good money selling marijuana. He was impressed that even though we were a part of that environment, we still didn't smoke weed. We knew people in the hood were making money from this, but we didn't jump on it because we were really afraid of the consequences of drug dealing. For every guy we saw making money from weed sales, we saw a lot more going to jail for the same. Before long, Big D invited us to smoke with him for free. We said no for a long time but eventually we gave in. The freebies were great. We would laugh, and listen to loud music from the big radios that Big D carried. But all the free fun came to an end after a couple of weeks. When we asked Big D to fire up one with us, he informed us, "Yo—it's time you purchase a bag." He laughed but he wasn't joking. If you wanted to smoke, you had pay for your own, because he was tired of supplying us for free.

We wanted the buzz but we didn't want to pay for it. I've heard that necessity is the mother of invention. At this point it was *necessary* for us to smoke, so we had to *invent* a way to get it done. The following week I decided that I would buy a large portion of marijuana, sell enough to get my money back and smoke the rest. This wasn't a course you could take in community college, and you couldn't go to your competition to ask for pointers. Drug dealing was a trade that was learned by trial and error and a lot of people I know have been to trial for making this error in judgment.

It wasn't long before my bankroll and my status in the hood started to grow along with my smoking habit. Hustling is in my blood, so I soon learned the trade. Money came in faster and in larger amounts. I went from purchasing half an ounce to purchasing ounces. Li'l Dave was more disciplined in his selling and saving. Dave became known as the self-proclaimed "Dime Bag King." We earned so much money that soon Dave and I both bought cars. Dave had a Lincoln Mark V. Mine was a Lincoln Town Car. I actually purchased two Town Cars and combined the parts to make one car. Ironically, one of the cars was the Lincoln I was almost killed in on the night of "Magnificent" Walt's chemical trip.

The Stinkin' Lincoln (as my two-toned love machine was called) immediately started to pay dividends in my popularity. My status with the young ladies began to rise also. The back seat of my Lincoln could testify to that. But all the time I was enjoying my new-found fame, lurking beneath the surface was my growing addiction to the marijuana and this crazy lifestyle. Before weed, an occasional Pink Champale would do to get my buzz on, but now it was the Champale with a reefer jay to chase. The reefer jays became the main course and my servings were larger than ever. One jay led to another. I found myself staying high all day. I sold the drugs to continually supply my habit and maintain my status in the hood.

Eventually, in the mid-eighties the marijuana game started to fade and I discovered a faster moneymaker. Cocaine was becoming more and more popular in Berkley. Cocaine dealing was the new dream job. No background check, no education requirements and definitely no drug screens. This was a no-brainer. *Where do I sign?* Li'l Dave and fellow Airplane Mikey were already involved on a small level, and just like before, they gave me some to try for free. Here I was again trying a drug, and once more, I became a slave to it.

It all started to steamroll one summer night in 1987, when "the devil himself" boarded a bus from New York City to Berkley. Chico, an old acquaintance of mine, arrived in Norfolk carrying a shoulder bag and in that bag was a vanilla wafer box. The citizens of Berkley would have been better off had that box contained only cookies. But hidden in the box were plummeting property values, prostitution, low self esteem and even murder.

Chico was my next door neighbor's nephew. He and I went way back. As a teenager, he and his brothers and cousins used to come to Norfolk every summer to visit. Even at a young age you could see he was trouble. When he came to town, everything stopped for me. From sun up 'til sun down, I was with Chico, whether we were pitching pennies against the curb, or listening to Lonnie, Chico's cousin, recite the lines of Rudy Ray Moore's *Signifyin' Monkey*.

We enjoyed each other's company. I didn't know that his visit this time was to start a company but it wasn't long before the picture was clear. Chico and I made the short trip from the Greyhound bus station to my house. When we got inside, Chico pulled a lump of something from the cookie box. As he tore off the plastic you could almost feel the trouble entering the neighborhood. The substance was so beautiful it almost looked like jewelry. It was cocaine, pure white with flakes like fish scales. This was it, the mother lode and if Chico had it, I knew I was down with it. That night turned into an all night get-high party, one of many which were to follow.

The next day Chico informed me that we were going to get rich. His sales pitch started with one big lie and the deceit never stopped coming. He made me believe that he was the man, that his resources were unlimited, and that he was in total control. He *wasn't* in control of the supply and neither was he in control of his expensive dope snorting and cocaine smoking habits. I paid no attention to his habit; I had a growing one of my own. More than that, I was only thinking about the money. By now fear of arrest, and any other thing that would stop me from this attempt at glory, had diminished. I was about to get my hustle on at a level none of my friends had ever seen. Local guys were selling fifteen-dollar and maybe fifty-dollar pieces of cocaine powder but we had hundred pieces, sixteenths and eightballs. Even if you needed a half ounce, Chico and Chico, Inc. had what you needed. I quickly became known as the person with the connections. What was really up for sale was my life and my soul.

Some people will try to tell you it is never as bad as it seems. If I had the chance to make the statement it would read "It is always as bad as it seems and even worse." If it walks like a duck, looks like a duck, and quacks like a duck, it's a duck. Another good way to do something about your situation is to tell yourself the truth about what you are going through. Sugarcoating the truth only gives you a false sense of security and may cause you not to put forth the immediate action needed to combat the problem.

It was told to me the first step in fixing a problem is to admit you have one. The problem should be measured for exactly what it is. There is no way you can look at a great big elephant and call it small. A problem should be surveyed, and assessed with extreme truth.

A big problem should be looked at as a big opportunity for a huge triumph. Although you may have a mammoth of a problem it doesn't mean instant defeat. It will take some time to dismiss this problem, but it can be done. An elephant can be eaten, only one bite at a time; like that elephant your problem or situation can be dissected, separated, and devoured. One bite at a time.

FIVE

When I think back to my grammar school experience, I can remember Pebeo's Circle. We impressionable children from the Park sat in a circle with our teacher wearing a cow puppet on her hand. It was like a show and tell. Ms. Oliver, using Pebeo the puppet, asked us questions. The topic one day was "What do you want to be when you grow up?" Hands darted in the air. All of the children were eager to give the class a peek into their shining futures. Ignorant of the skills and knowledge we'd need to achieve these goals, and unaware of the slim chances that children from our background had to ever realize our dreams, we made our career choices known. Tiny voices blurted out Lawyer! Doctor! And my choice, Pro football player! Without hesitation. Basketball player! Scientist! Teacher! much to the pleasure of Ms. Oliver. No child in the circle ever mentioned that he or she wanted to grow up to be a drug addict or an alcoholic, but here it was years later and I was both. When I was in the fifth grade I was the best reader in my class. My teacher Ms. Davis would prophesize that I would have an office job and the rest of the class would be working for me. At this point, boy, was she wrong.

All my dreams and aspirations had dissolved like crack on the hot stem of a crack pipe. My mother had gotten tired of my antics and moved from the house at 1002 leaving me and my brother and sister to fend for ourselves. They also were dabbling in drugs and alcohol. History had repeated itself. Just as she got tired and left my father, she got tired and left me. I bought the house from the landlord and handled my destructive lifestyle from there.

As the word started to spread that I was able to get good cocaine, Jabba Jaws became a household name among the Get-high Circle. Between the fast rate I was moving the drugs and our own growing habits it was hard for Chico and me to keep product. We'd make unauthorized runs to New York. I thought we were just visiting his family but Chico was cutting deals to bring back drugs. He was trying to hide his mishandling of the drugs from his brother-in-law "B," so he'd sneak to New York and score without B's knowledge. I realized that Chico was not in fact "The Man." He was only working for B, one of the scariest men I had ever met in my life. B used intimidation to keep his business going and one look from him would strike fear in your heart. B demonstrated his fury one day when he found that Chico had product that wasn't the same as B had given to him and Chico tried to convince B that it *was*. B stormed though the house screaming his displeasure. He took the drugs Chico had, dumped them in the toilet, flushed them and gave Chico a stern warning never to do it again. I didn't know what Chico was going to do but I knew *I* would never make that trip again. Even though this was a horrifying event, I was too far in the drug game to stop now.

I was serving the street dealers but soon that changed. The more I sold the more interest B had in my dealings. It wasn't long before he knew all my customers by name. Eventually he no longer needed me and he dealt directly to my customers. I was angry but I wasn't about to challenge B. This brother had told us a story about being shot in the head and driving himself to the hospital on a motorcycle. Legend had it he rode the motorcycle right through the glass doors with the bullet still in his head. I thought, *My God, this man is crazy.* After he took over my customers, my consolation was a measly half-ounce to hit the streets with and sell on my own. This was the beginning of my downward spiral into failure as a drug dealer.

Nevertheless, my addiction was progressing. What started out as an occasional Pink Champale monkey on my back had grown into a crack cocaine Mighty Joe Young-size gorilla. I would snort to get my package ready and snort after the bagging up process was done. My habit grew with each package. I snorted powder all day long. I can remember snorting so much that my nose would no longer receive the drug. It was like I lost the power to snort. I would try to sniff it up my nostrils and the cocaine would fall right back out. An occasional nose bleed still wouldn't stop me from trying to get the cocaine in my nose. Sometime when I would sniff the drug in my nose the pain would be excruciating. Sometimes I would lie back and pour coke into my nose and dampen it with water so that I could get the drain off the coke down my throat. I dreaded blowing my nose because what seemed like my sinuses would come out my nostrils and I would have to sniff them back up into my head. My nose would bleed during these episodes but I continued to use. I was gone. One night I used so much that my heart started to race. It scared me so bad that I walked down to my mother's house and lay on her floor. I wanted to be around my mom just in case I died.

I still continued my destructive behavior. It was like I was possessed by some madman who would not be satisfied until I killed myself. I would try to hide my growing addiction from others. I had ignored the first rule of dealing, "Don't get high off your own supply." I was my own biggest customer. I lived to get high and got high to live.

By this time I was totally convinced I was in trouble. I started using so much that even the little guys I had in the street dealing were skipping past me and seeking B for themselves. I used more than I sold.

My crack cocaine habit started in 1988, one night when I was one on one with Chico. We had been selling and getting high all day. We were at the end of our package and we decided to use what was left ourselves. I ran out of powder to toot and Chico suggested I try his custom-made crack pipe. It was a small cardboard roll that came off the bottom of a hanger from the cleaners. The cardboard had a hole cut in the top on one end and was wrapped in aluminum foil. Chico had used the pipe so often that the cardboard was saturated with cocaine. In fact it was so saturated that he could pluck at the tube and residue from the pipe would come out. He would smoke the residue. After taking my first blast off the pipe I was in love. Head over heels. Lost and didn't care. She was beautiful Ms. Crack. She was dressed to kill. So fine I would drink her bath water. I thought I had been in love before but not like this. I was sprung. Nothing in the world mattered but getting another hit. I smoked with Chico until there was no crack left. I was so messed up that later that night I stole Chico's pipe. The next morning I took it to my mother's house, unraveled it and smoked the paper tube itself. Life as I knew it was over. I was on a mission and Scotty could beam me up anytime. Chico was proving my theory that surely he was the devil or at least they were on a first name basis.

I was smoking, but I didn't want anyone to know. The only one I would smoke around was Chico. One day, after I had been smoking a couple of weeks, my younger brother Doo-Wop came into the house where I was getting high. I tried to hide it by not smoking in front of him, but he told me he already knew I was smoking. The news that he knew hurt me a little because I respected Doo-Wop, and I didn't want him to know that I was out there like this. Doo-Wop's finding out liberated me, because once he knew I couldn't care less about who else in the street knew. But I never wanted the news of my smoking to reach my mom.

The news finally did reach her. The house that I purchased was starting to go down. Lights were off; so was the water. We flushed the toilet with water we borrowed from neighbors. I had gradually started to live at my mother's apartment down the street.

I'd leave her house on Wednesday, hit the street to get high, living from crackhouse to crackhouse, and return to her house on Sunday. During those days I rarely got sleep nor did I eat much. One day while I was resting from my weekend binge, my ex-girlfriend Shana sat down on the bed beside me at my mothers' house. We had broken up but she was still close to the family. She asked me what was up with me. After a few minutes of questioning, I finally made a confession. Not only was this confession news to Shana, but it was also news to me. I told her, *I think I have a drug problem*. I tried desperately to get her to keep it to herself. She eventually told my mother.

Up to that point, I didn't think it was a drug *problem*, but I was starting to see the effects. I was in the street all night long. I had begun to lose weight and I had started to look rough. My skin started to darken, my weight was decreasing and my hygiene was horrible. I remember that when I started this journey I had earned a GED and started Commonwealth College. I had a trade doing body repair and painting cars. Now all of these things were in jeopardy because I had no control over my life.

I could see all the bad news this drug was bringing but I continued my subscription. I was still going to Commonwealth and to church but I was selling drugs, too. I had to make a decision—either stay in church and school and have money in the future, or keep selling drugs and get money *now*. I decided to chase the dragon and here I was a slave in the dragon's castle with no way out. It was official: Byron "Jabba Jaws" Joyce was a crackhead.

My drug abuse eventually led me back to my old address at 811 City Hall Avenue. The drug game was getting more wide open in Berkley. Rival drug gangs started moving into the community and B wanted to keep the action coming through him. By now, the drug game had turned people who used to be friends into foes. Mikey had started to score from another source. He and a few of his nephews had set up shop on South Main Street. B wanted them out of that location so he gave me, Chico, and Bubba (later to be known as Chico, Chico, and Chico) a large quantity of drugs to give away to keep the customers coming to us. We didn't give it away, but we sold it cheap and big.

So Mikey and his crew had to shut down. Some time later, Bubba, Chico, and I were standing on the corner celebrating our victory. Little Cherry, one of Mikey's nephews, came by and said that we'd better get off that corner. Thinking he was telling us to leave or they would *make* us leave, we told him we weren't going anywhere. Little did we know that his words were not a threat but a warning.

A few minutes later a car turned the corner. The car had the headlights turned off. At first it looked like a drive-by shooting developing. The car headed straight for us. Unmarked and without any flashing lights the car drew closer. After a few seconds we knew it was the police. Bubba and Chico went one way and I went another. Just my luck, the police chose me to follow. The police car accelerated and so did I. I made my way to the apartment building across the street. I entered the hallway and tried the door, but it was locked. The officers entered the hallway, seized me, and started their search. I had dropped what little drugs I had on me while entering the building. The officer pulled a fresh bottle of Canadian Mist from my pocket; originally, I was getting ready to celebrate the evening's events. This discovery would not put me in jail, but just as I started to think I was getting away, another officer entered the hallway with the bags I had discarded and announced, "Look what I found!" My heart dropped. Quickly I tried to say the drugs were not mine. My words meant nothing the officers and they started to read me my rights. The arrest was made right in front of my older sister, who was living in the apartment. I can remember standing there so embarrassed as my sister looked on.

The officers placed me in the car. Tight handcuffs held my hands together in the back seat of the patrol car. The officers took an unfamiliar route to the precinct. I had heard of police officers making arrests and taking the accused to a remote place and beating them before they took them to jail. I was afraid that maybe that might be the case. But the police took me to a new receiving center. Within minutes I was at my destination, "Heartbreak Hotel." After I was booked, I was transferred back to 811 City Hall Ave. Back to the place of burning sheets. It had been ten years since I'd been there and it hadn't changed any. The stench of dry piss wasn't amusing now, either. On one hand, I was not thrilled to be back in this place of despair and there was nothing good about it. But on the other hand I was happy I made it in one piece.

Sometimes when it seems like things have all gone to hell, it could be a blessing in disguise. The bad things that happen as a result of your problem or problems should serve as wake-up calls. If nothing ever went wrong you never would change. The setbacks may hurt and cost you dearly but you should accept them and use them to deter you from your negative behaviors. If it weren't for the bad things that happened to me I probably would still be smoking crack. My whippings, bad deals, and jail stays helped me to recognize that I needed a change. If your decisions are continuing to produce negative consequences, "check yourself before you wreck yourself."

SIX

My mother always said, "A hard head makes a soft behind." By now my behind was as soft as they come, and getting softer every minute. I disobeyed all the warnings. Hey, SAY NO TO DRUGS was printed everywhere—billboards, TV, candy boxes—it was everywhere and yet drugs had me. Byron Joyce, the peoples' choice. Ms. Davis's hand picked most likely to succeed candidate, a self-proclaimed pro football phenom in Pebeo's circle, strung out with no relief in sight. I was a young man with no direction and no purpose and the only thing I truly desired was another hit on the crack can. Any can would do—big cans, small cans, old cans, new cans—it didn't make a difference. I've used a small pepper can and I've used a miniature beer keg. By now smoking and drinking had totally possessed my life. My drug habit would cause me to take on the role of many characters and bring me to death's door on several occasions.

I made a phone call to Chico and within a few hours I was back on the street. He and Bubba came to bond me out. While headed to the vehicle I made two requests—stop me by Hardee's to get a burger and get me to the crib so that I can take a blast and get a stiff drink. I had to have it. Canadian Mist and cocaine were like bacon and eggs, Michael and Scotty, Laurel and Hardy; for me they just went together. Cocaine picked me up and the drink would mellow me out. I loved it. I had no job, no steady girl, a deteriorating relationship with my family but, still, I wanted to get high. Before the burger had time to touch down in my belly I was smoking again.

My habit was expensive. I smoked big rocks, at least a twenty-dollar piece (street value), every time I fired up. I sold so much that I could afford this type of binge. I know I used enough drugs to represent the gross national product of a few small countries. At first I was being fed kibbles and bits by Chico, but after I got tired of his conniving I set out on my own. I started to smoke twenty-four hours a day, from Wednesday to Sunday morning non-stop. I would pass out on Sunday and wake up Monday to resume the madness. Monday and Tuesday were slow days for dealing so I didn't smoke as much, but Wednesday would start the circus all over again. Circus it was and I was the ringmaster. Not only did I get me high but all the people around me enjoyed the benefits of my habit. All the other crackheads wanted to work with me because they knew that I was going to keep them high. "Gernt" Elliot who made money so fast it used to amaze me. When I went independent he was my right hand man. The crew began to grow. Pincy, Mike Geddes, and even Mike Ferguson, a former mailman-turned-crackhead-turned-Jabba's-independent-crack-distributor, were just a few of the people that helped me supply my habit.

Donnie "Icky Boo" Mann also joined the crew. This was the same Icky who hit a guy so hard in the Thanksgiving Day football game that the guy went to his car and got his pistol and warned Donnie not to ever hit him like that again or he would shoot him. Donnie, who was well-respected in the hood as an athlete and fighter, was now just a crackhead. Donnie had gotten to the point that he was selling dummy crack to people. Dummy crack was anything that even slightly resembled crack. Rocks, soap, or peanuts would do. He used to sell to a customer on one corner, run through the alley, change clothes and sell another dummy to the same dummy on another corner. I convinced him that he might be safer selling for me. Although he had my real dope he still sold dummies and smoked the real crack himself.

I used to take over people's houses just by getting them high. One girl's habit was so strong I decided to pay her cash to move out of her own house. She was paid fifty dollars a day for weekdays and seventy-five dollars for Friday and Saturday. It was cheaper for me than letting her smoke.

Even though I was a fiend I still had some principles, and I expected the people around me to have principles, too. I'm reminded of a time when Chuck Whitehurst approached me to buy crack. He only had eight dollars and seventy-five cents. I promised him that my package was on the way and if he gave me what he had I would look out for him. Some time later the package arrived. I was told that Chuck was still waiting on the sidewalk. I was surprised he was still there. I shouted from the apartment, "Chuck, if you don't have that eight dollars and seventy-five cents you ain't getting nothing." The thing was, he already had short money but I wasn't going to tolerate a penny less. We made a deal for eight seventy-five and that was the only deal I would accept.

Principle was important, One day Raymond Harper showed he had none and I just about lost my mind. The night before I had gotten him high, gave him work and brought him a pair of brand-new sneakers. We made a pact to hustle together the next day. When morning came he was working with someone else. All I could think was *I just bought this nigga a pair of sneakers and he gonna cross me.* I walked up to Ray and we discussed the situation rather loudly in front of the crowd on Stafford Street. At the conclusion of our debate, I demanded my shoes back. He wouldn't give them up so I pulled my pistol. I cocked the gun and fired a shot near his feet and asked for the shoes again. He refused; I fired another shot. This time I told him "My next shot is going in my shoes." He immediately kicked the shoes off. It wasn't the shoes, it was the *principle* of the whole matter. The code of the street was a man is only as good as his word. I tried really hard to keep principle. My principles helped me even to have good relationships with those who could keep me supplied.

I was making money on a large scale in late '88. Berkley was jumping and the customers loved me. I could grind a thousand dollars in a couple of hours. My customers were loyal; they would walk past other dealers to get to me. Still I never really saw the benefits of the money. But the people supplying me were getting ghetto rich. B and Li'l Dave had trucks, BMWs, and houses and I had a smoking can. I was hooking up with other drug sources and making bigger profits.

The more I made the more I smoked and smoked and smoked.

When I got an opportunity to get down with "C" it was full speed ahead. C was a young ambitious dealer who had also came from NYC. I learned he was paying crackheads twenty dollars for every hundred dollars they turned in. I jumped on that deal. At first everything ran okay, then I met Ronald.

Ronald was about fifteen years old when we met. He came to me and asked me to give him some work. I hesitated because he was so young and I didn't want to involve him in this vicious game. *Look at what it had done to me.* But Ronald was persistent. One day I took him up on his offer. I gave him a job just taking the crack package to the house while I followed from a distance. When we got to the house I would pay him a few bucks. This wasn't enough for Ronald so he started to sell for other dealers. I immediately hunted him down and made him a part of my team. Ronald was a beast; next to me he was the best hustler that ever done it. One night Ronald took one hundred dollars' worth of crack out of the house to serve a customer. He came back with $275 and some of the crack left. He was the man.

We sold so much crack that one night I went in to collect my commission from C's New York crew. They checked the books and they owed me $800. One of C's crew, protested strongly. He called C on the phone and said, "God, I am *not* giving this man no eight hundred."

C wanted to talk to me. He said, "Jaws, you know we only pay crackheads like that."

I retorted, "What am I, then?"

After much deliberation we agreed to a four-hundred dollar buyout. The next day C hit me with a bonus package so that was cool, but after that he found it more economical to just give me a package and not pay the commission. Ronald had single-handedly turned my business up another level.

Ronald paved the way for two other young scramblers, Hog and Li'l Cherry. All these guys were around the same age. When Ronald brought these guys around I found out from people in the street Ronald was smoking crack, too. Ronald and Hog would get lost on a regular basis. They always made the money, but they stayed high. Hog began to slow down Ronald's production so I encouraged Ronald to distance himself.

Li'l Cherry was a character. This boy had no shame. He was getting high and he didn't care who knew it. Cherry would do what he had to do to get his crack. I walked into one of the houses I was running and saw Cherry sitting there with a gun to his head and a can in his mouth. He wouldn't move until I gave him a blast of cocaine. He kept an imaginary girl and dog with him that he talked to all the time. He would walk in the front door after taking customers' money outside, score and walk out the back door and leave the customer with nothing. When the customer would catch up with Cherry he would pull his pistol and dare the customer to try him. Sometimes he would have a piece of wood in a bag and pretend it was a gun.

Cherry would try anybody, even me. One night he stood at the end of the alley with his gun, daring me to come outside. He was mad because I wouldn't let him come in to get high with the crew. I sent someone out to distract him as I ran around the building and came up from his blind side as he was walking away. I stuck my pistol in his face and he broke down.

"Daddy, don't shoot! Please daon't shoot."

I never wanted to hurt him, but respect was a huge part of the street code.

The rival dealers hated us. I was known as the "Discount Man," the Wal-Mart of crack dealers. If you sold it for twenty I'd take fifteen. Every day, my life had drama and sometimes my life was on the line. One day I was approached by two fellows. Jay, Chico's cousin, who was supposed to be down with me, was jealous of my crew and figured if I was erased my crew would soon follow. The two emerged from Jay's car, one with a .45 revolver, the other packing a TEC-9 submachine gun. Jay announced, "Your 'Discount Man' days are over."

I just knew I was a goner. Both of these guys were known to shoot folks and I thought I was the next on their list of victims. They accused me of robbing one of them the night before. I removed my jewelry, gave it up and all the contents of my pockets, too. One of the gunmen asked why I was giving up my stuff if I didn't do it. I answered, "If this will keep me alive, take it."

They took the spoils and got back in the car without firing a shot, much to the displeasure of Jay. Jay never did like me. Once he tried to get me to walk in a dark field with him after accusing me of robbing his man. I said, "If you gonna shoot me you'll do it in front of witnesses 'cause I'm not going anywhere."

That was just the beginning. "Cheese," another dealer, after having a beef with me, fired shots at my car. Seymour and Piper, more dealers, hunted me for weeks or at least I thought they did. I was run out of Oakleaf Park to the tune of thunderous gunfire. Once when B heard I was scoring drugs from other places, he too decided to unleash his anger upon Jabba. He entered a house I was selling out of one Saturday morning, gun in hand, and expressed his displeasure with what he heard I was doing. I was horrified. He grabbed my drugs and flushed them down the toilet. If he didn't do anything else to me; this move was damage enough. I thought, *What's wrong with this guy, is he gotta keep flushing my drugs down the toilet?* He started shouting "This shop is closed!"

I didn't disagree at all. What was I to say? He had a gun and this was Bullet-in-the-Head B. He waved the pistol and yelled "This shop is closed." Again I seconded his motion, "No problem—it's *closed*!"

I would have done anything short of a sexual act just to make him leave and not shoot. But B said, "I have to do *something* to you." He pointed the pistol in my direction and dropped his hand as he pulled the trigger. The bullet ricocheted off the floor and hit the wall. He came at me with the gun and swung at my head. I ducked the first blow but I didn't want him to shoot me so the next time he tried to hit me I took the blow. I felt warm blood rolling down the back of my neck. I was so scared I never felt the pain. I looked at him, grabbed my wound and said, "You say shop closed, SHOP CLOSED!"

B left the house and I went to the restroom to nurse my wound. While I was in the restroom B came back with a baseball bat. He swung it before I knew he was there. All of a sudden, the baseball bat struck the door jamb. The noise was so loud I thought I had been shot. I looked back to see it was B. I grabbed the bat and screamed, "Shop closed, man, shop *closed*!"

We struggled for the bat, and after a couple of minutes he ran out. This time I could sense something was strange, so instead of waiting for another attack I jumped out the window and ran down the street. I was no more than a block away when I heard shots fired. The shots were rapid and abundant. No doubt B had come back to shoot me. When and if I make it to heaven I'll be looking for that awesome angel, who kept his wings around me.

Even though the drugs were causing me all this trouble, I still continued to smoke. On the day when I was supposed to report to court on my possession charge, where was I? Smoking. I didn't make it to court and a failure to appear charge was added to my case. I was out on bail so this prompted the bondman to revoke my bond and send the bounty hunters to find me. I had heard someone was asking about my whereabouts, but I never thought it was law enforcement. I figured it was just a customer looking for the Discount Man.

One morning, after selling everything I had the night before, including black rock that was made from the residue of my crack can, I went marching through the street acting a fool. I was high; I walked to South Main Street to look for more drugs to buy. I stopped to talk with a girl sitting on her porch. I looked one hot mess, but because I was so high, I thought I was the bomb. I was standing there dressed in unlaced sneakers, no socks, and a pair of shorts with no shirt. I was skinny, head knotty, ankles dirty, but I was Jabba. I bent over waving my arms and shuffling my feet. While in the act of trying to convince the girl to cheat on her boyfriend, I was the victim of a sneak attack. A bounty hunter came up from behind and slapped the handcuffs on me. Not only did he arrest me but he conned me into giving him my money. I was arrested and robbed all at the same time. The consequence of my skipping court was serious. I was given a bond but no bondsman wanted to touch me at first and that meant I had to remain in jail. And the worst part of that was in jail there was no crack.

After a couple of attempts to get a bondsman, one finally showed interest in my case. He let me know that the only way he might consider bonding me out was for my mother to sign for me. I immediately put in a call to her to make the request. My mother is a good woman. Her whippings bordered on child abuse, but still she was a decent woman.

"BY-Y-Y-ron," she said in her southern dialect, "I much rather you be in that jail where you're safe and I know where you are, than have you in this street with all these horror stories I hear about you."

My mother was right, so I set up to stay until my trial. She had a change of heart and she came to get me after a few days. She made a stipulation that I attend some meetings at the church. I agreed because I wanted out in the worst way. After I was released on bond I was supposed to go see this probation lady. My father (yes, my father, the main blame in this ongoing saga) and I sat there for a while but my patience was short and we left. Leaving would prove to be another of the many mistakes I made in my life.

I did the right thing for a while after I was bailed out. I stayed in the house, and even attended a couple of support group meetings. The days were long and tough. I lasted maybe a week before I crossed Berkley Avenue. I was high before my feet touched the ground on the other side of the street. My body was craving so bad I felt like I had a hit already. When I reached Stafford Street the fiends greeted me with open arms. They couldn't wait to give me a hit to get started because they knew when I got started the party was on again.

I would wind up in trouble again with the law. I made a call to the probation officer three days or so after my release. She blasted me on the phone. She demanded that I come to her office right away. I was already high and I knew if I showed at the lady's office she was going to send me to jail. There was no way I was leaving my crack can again. I never showed up and once again I was a fugitive.

This time I knew they would send the bounty hunters and I was prepared. All the time my habit was getting worse. I was really looking bad in the game. I went from the up-and-coming man to somebody I couldn't even recognize. I still had my pride and I didn't want people to laugh, so I turned my crack smoking into one big joke. Every day I was doing something crazy. At one point I even started dressing in costume. This tactic was partially to duck the bounty hunters but mostly to feel like people were laughing with me and not at me.

The costumes were a sure sign of a genius or a maniac. I would dress up in a bumblebee suit, mini skirt and wig, vines wrapped around my entire body with a leafy tree limb in front of me to hide my face. I'd hold the limb in front of me and take baby steps on my tiptoes like the wolf on the cartoon, occasionally peeking out from behind the bush and amusing my street audience. I remember one night when I came out the house wrapped in a white sheet with a lampshade on my head. I had a lighter tucked under the lampshade and a string around my neck. If you wanted to buy something I'd tell you to pull the string and I'd light the lighter and fill your prescription. Dressed in a dress and wig, I sold crack out of a baby stroller.

One day I dressed like Moses, staff, beard and sandals. I strode down Stafford Street, one of the busiest drug spots at that time. I slowly approached a well-known gambling spot and walked in. I stood there, raised my arms and my staff and then turned and walked out. Standing on the porch, I was approached by a fellow who observed that I was always doing something crazy. I pointed my staff at his car and told him, "Shut up before I part that car in half!"

When he went to start his car it wouldn't start, and he was *furious*.

My mother came up on me one day while I was dressed in a long trench coat and a big hat with a walkie talkie held to my mouth. She looked and called my name, then called it again. Finally I turned to her and said in a low voice "Shhh—I'm undercover."

She looked at me as if I had driven a stake through her heart. I was trying to play it off but her pain was my pain. I didn't want to be strung out. I didn't want to be in the street with no future but here I was. My self-respect was gone and I didn't have a clue how to get it back.

My costumes kept me out of jail for a while. Those crazy antics kept police off my trail. They thought I was crazy and maybe I was. Many a day I saw them look at me, shake their heads in pity and move on. The bounty hunters didn't have a clue. The tables had been turned. Before they knew what I looked like and I didn't know who they were. Now, I knew them but they never could tell what I would dress as that day. Once while standing on the corner with my fake beard and afro wig on, the bounty hunter who robbed me drove right past me. He drove for about a block and then put the car in reverse. He looked at me again and said accusingly, "I thought you were going to turn yourself in."

I answered, "I will, but not today," and away I ran. Again I had escaped the bounty hunter and my disguise was the reason I got away.

The disguises couldn't fool everybody. The day after Easter I was down on Stafford Street. It was a Monday so money was slow. I was waiting for the next sell to come when a police car turned. I had on my afro wig to disguise my look. Just so happened one of the officers that was in the cruiser was the same cop that arrested me on my original charge. As I started to walk away the car moved toward me to cut off my path. I ran into the hallway and entered a friend's apartment. She was the local drama queen who doubled as a crackhead. I told her, "Don't open that door!"

The police convinced her otherwise. By now I was in the bedroom in the bed buck naked. I had thrown my wig and my clothes in the closet. The officer came in the room and ordered "Man, get up from there!"

I sprang from under the covers in my birthday suit. He made me get dressed and led me from the apartment.

The night before my arrest I had gone to my mother's house. She asked me if I was going to turn myself in. I told her that I didn't want to be in jail during the summer so I'd wait until fall and then I'd surrender. She didn't argue; she just kissed me and I left the house. It was like a kiss of death. I thought about that kiss all the way down the street. The next day I was under arrest.

I was headed back to the place of rehab, 811 City Hall Avenue. The rooms of locked-up potential and a graveyard of hope, with two crack rocks stuck in the cavities in my teeth. I smoked the rocks in the holding cell that night. I was arrested and sitting in the city jail for the fourth time. I was skinny, dirty, and strung out. Something had to change and I was ready for it.

The bottom is the place people reach when they realize that their situation is about as bad as it gets. When it seems nothing is going right. When the hole that you have dug for yourself makes you feel that there is no relief in sight. By now friends have turned their backs on you, family don't want to be associated with you and you don't even like yourself.

The bottom is a place of great thinking and little hope. Most time in this place of despair, drastic measures are taken and a lot of tears are shed. Doubt is your closest companion and confidence is at an all time low.

For me, at my bottom, quitting was not an option. Something had to be done and if it was to be it was up to me. Someone told me that "no one can stop me but me." I was my worst enemy, not crack, not the streets, but me. In the bottom you have to own up to what you created. You can't justify your mess. My pastor says "admit it and quit it." The bottom may become a part of your life. Even the best of us can go there, but "bottom" doesn't have to be a permanent address.

SEVEN

Hell (hel) *n.* 1. *Any place or condition of great evil, torment or misery.*

You know, looking back, I had to be the stupidest man on earth. I had chosen to care about everything but what mattered most, myself. I had found myself a walking corpse in a living hell. I could see the devil's work all over my situation. I was burning in pain and I was the cause. Even though lots of people had their hands in the development of this photo, it was time for me to take responsibility for the ugly image that was revealed. A change needed to be made and if it was going to happen, it was up to me.

Man, my fourth trip to lock up and you know what? Rightfully so. Though I had done a few things in my life that I was proud of, overall I was still a bum. Yeah, I had obtained my GED after being thrown out of school. Sure, I had gone to trade school and received my papers for auto body repair. So what? I bought my first house at twenty-five but I still had a crack habit, no job, and no plans for the future. I was batting a thousand.

The brothers in jail were glad to see me. They acknowledged that I had a good run, meaning that I had stayed out for a while. Though they were happy to greet me this was the last sight I wanted to see.

After a few days of just sleeping and eating I gained enough strength to stay awake. I sat in a makeshift tent that I had constructed on the floor in the corner of the cell. I had not been assigned a bunk yet so I had to sleep on a mattress on the floor. I had ordered a deck of cards from the canteen and I marked them under the tent. I used the marked cards to beat fellow inmates out of cigarettes. Cigarettes were the currency used to buy favors throughout the jail.

After a few days the effect of the crack was starting to wear off. I was beginning to see the truth about my life. I knew jail was never my plan. So I traced my path back to the place where it all started to go to hell. The separation of my parents played a big role in this Kodak moment. It wasn't only the split, but also the lack of involvement on my father's part. Even though he had never put any effort into my upbringing before, I still kind of hoped he would come around to being the Ward Cleaver-type father that I saw on TV. Nevertheless he was my dad and I wanted my father in my life despite his inconsistencies. I thought about this little song that I made up. The song was about how *father* was a name I used to call and *momma* was a name I didn't want to call. I blamed my mother for the break up but that was a little twisted. Looking back, if she was guilty of anything it was trying to get something better for us.

I started to write a letter in the sanctuary of that tent. It was a letter to my younger brother Doo-Wop who was locked up on another floor. The message in the letter was that we had to stop punishing ourselves for the mistakes that our parents made. The letter had no real effect on my brother, for he continued his life of crime and wound up doing a long bid in penitentiary. But for me, that letter was the spark that started a fire of recovery. One day a guy came by the cell with some religious literature.. He was praying for the inmates. I stuck my head out for him to pray for me too. I didn't know if it would do any good, but what did I have to lose?

I found myself content with the time I had to spend in jail. Bail was out of the question with all the shenanigans I had pulled on bail bondsmen, so I just made the best of my situation. I started a little casino with a pair of dice I got from the next cell over and the cards I ordered from the canteen. I received a cut from the dice games and the card games. My profits kept fried chicken, pizza, omelets and other specialties from the jailhouse kitchen coming. The hall man would make purchases for you and deliver them for a small fee. The meals were great but I still needed something more. I was locked up, but my mind was far from that cell.

Before now, my mind would be on getting out and getting high again but this time I really didn't want any crack. I wasn't shy about sharing the news that I didn't want to smoke any more. Chico was housed in the cell next to mine. I told him that when I got out I was going to make all the money I could but I didn't want to smoke anything. His response was, "More for me." He added, "When I get out of here I'm going to hit the biggest blast I can find."

Even though he still wanted to get toasted it had no effect on my decision. I was starting to feel a sense of change.

It hit home one day while I was sitting in my cell. The kitchen people came to serve us lunch. Bananas were on the menu, and they handed them to us through the bars. That really got under my skin. I was already ticked off because I wanted a burger so bad and I had no way of getting one. Now here I was taking a banana through bars like a monkey. I was convinced that this love affair with foolishness was over. *I am never coming to this place again.* A small voice spoke back to me within seconds. The message it had was pure and precise. *If you smoke again you will be back.* My answer was swift and direct. *Well, I'm not smoking anymore.* I didn't have a clue how I was going to achieve this goal, but I meant what I said. I no longer wanted to come back to that place of degradation. I no longer wanted to dress up in costumes or wear the same clothes for weeks. I didn't want to keep my ankles so dirty that even after a good washing they still weren't clean. I hated the fact that I was living from pillar to post, losing weight, and rarely seeing my family. I was no longer happy about being shot at, shooting at people or being the victim of every crackhead joke you can think of. I was sick and tired of being sick and tired and I didn't care who knew it.

Later that night, while sitting on the benches and chatting with some of my fellow inmates, we started to tap on the tables and start a free-style rap session. I ripped the mike with my free-style rap (meaning I spoke rhymes to the rhythm). The hook to the song was "I'm Gonna Drop the Can." The song was about my decision to stop smoking crack and stop coming back to jail. Another guy broke out singing "I shall wear a crown" and the whole mood of the cell, at least in my mind, was changed.

The nights didn't even seem to be long anymore. Normally I would be bugging about getting out of jail, now it was different. I was content with my surroundings and I wasn't in a hurry to leave. Still I had to face the charges that I was arrested for, but somehow that didn't press me either. The one thing I wanted to do was never return to this hell and the way I had to do that was to SAY NO TO DRUGS.

You know what; God must be a really nice guy, because even in the midst of your mess there is an escape somewhere. A crack with a sliver of light—if you can just get through it you will be all right.

I just can't imagine someone who would still offer an alternative plan for some of the garbage we get ourselves in. If I were him, I probably would have hit myself with a lightning bolt. Some of you probably feel the same. The truth is if you are going to make it out of your situation you are going to have to believe that you still matter. Yes, you've messed up; yes, you are in a lot of trouble; yes, your momma and nem can't stand you right now, but even in the midst of that, you matter.

The word salvation *is related to the word* salvage. *The act of salvage is performed when someone goes into a wreckage, finds something of value, cleans it up and uses it for a purpose. Right now it may not look or feel good but there is something in your wreckage of a life that is worth saving. Old bleach bottles become new flower pots. Old tires become new swings. You never know how your story is going to turn out, so don't give up. This is not the time to throw in the towel. Even though you tore up from the floor up, God's a nice guy.*

EIGHT

In the story of David and Goliath, nobody really believed that David would overcome the nine-foot, nine-inch giant. Some of his comrades were probably betting against him. Legend has it that David put the giant down with one of the five smooth stones he had collected by the brook. I too was facing a giant, the giant of addiction, not only to drugs but also to the lifestyle.

Jail wasn't a place I wanted to be, but I was safe there. In jail I didn't have to worry about the temptation of hitting the street to make a dollar selling crack. I didn't have to worry about the temptation of taking a hit of cocaine. No one was shooting at me in the jail. Jail was a sanctuary for me but I couldn't stay there forever. Yes, my Goliaths were real and I knew that upon my release they would be standing at the gate waiting for me.

I was held in jail until my trial date in May, 1990. I had already been tried on a gun charge and driving without a license in another courtroom. I was found guilty but the time I had served leading up to my trial paid that sentence. Then I was led to the Circuit Court, Courtroom Nine. As I entered the courtroom, the first recognizable face I saw was my mother's. She sat there with that *Boy, I told you so, but I hope you'll be all right*, look on her face. Next to her was the Reverend

Jake Manley, the founder of the Showers of Blessings program at Bethany Baptist Church. I had attended the program a couple of times, but I wasn't seeking help then; I was just going though the motions to please my mom. I was seated at the table with a court-appointed attorney who kept urging me to plead guilty. At one point during the trial I told him to not say anything. He was acting like he had an appointment, and he wanted to get rid of me as soon as possible so he could keep it. My thoughts were, *When he leaves, I'm leaving, too.* Even though I was not in control I was determined not to spend another day in that place. I had rehearsed my story and I was sticking with it.

The trial started and the police officer was asked to take the stand. He testified about the night in question and amazingly, he told it like it was. He didn't lie on me to help his case, and if my crack-fried brain serves me correctly he even gave me credit for being cooperative during the arrest. He must have had good notes because the initial arrest had taken place quite some time ago. I had been through a many a bondsman and bounty hunter since the initial arrest. The officer stepped down from the witness stand and it was my turn to test-a-lie.

My story was just like the officer's. I was careful to match key points in the officer's testimony; I just left out the part about dropping the drugs on the ground. I also added that I was going to (if allowed), get a job and enroll in college. Rev. Manley testified that the church was willing to help get my life on track. I can't remember if my mother took the stand, but there is one thing in the trial that I'll never forget. The judge made the most profound statement in the whole trial. She was a seasoned white woman, Lydia Taylor. Judge Taylor calmly told me, "Mr. Joyce, I am going to find you guilty of possession of cocaine and sentence you to five years." When she said that everything just stopped. Time stood still. What was only a few seconds seemed like ten minutes. My heart dropped and an already quiet courtroom got quieter.

The judge's next words were the key to saving my life. She said she was going to suspend the sentence and place me on probation for five years. She went on to ask me, "Mr. Joyce, were they your drugs?" and I 'fessed up.

She said "Mr. Joyce, you don't need a job, nor do you need to be trying to get in school. You just need to get yourself together."

When she said that, it was like she took the weight of the world off my shoulders. I knew exactly what she meant; I needed to leave drugs alone forever. If I got that straight I would be all right. If I could resist the pressures of getting high, success would possibly be mine. No job, no school, no trying to impress people, no pressure to be great, just be clean and sober. I guess the judge was part of the crazy angel package that I had throughout this whole foolish episode in my life.

Within thirty minutes, I was released from Norfolk City Jail for the last time. Except for probation, I was free. I was ready to make the adjustments I needed to live a successful life. I knew what I wanted but I didn't have any clue how I was going to get it done.

Sherry picked me up from the jailhouse. She was a young lady who used to buy drugs from me. I developed an attraction to her and we started to spend time together. Before I went to jail, Sherry stayed with her sister in an apartment on State Street. The apartment was away from the central area where I did my dirt. I would use their place for a spot to chill and hide out. Sherry soon became pregnant with twins. After I was locked up, she went to stay at her adopted mother's house in Virginia Beach. Because she was pregnant by me, her mother allowed me to move in with them when I was released. We left the jail and rode through Berkley. It was like entering a land of make-believe. The trees looked so green and the air even smelled fresher. Looking back I know that it was my addiction playing tricks on me.

I made it out of Berkley's trap that day. I made it to a couple of meetings including a Showers of Blessings Meeting. This was the first time I met Gerald. Big Gerald was a former addict who worked for the local rehabilitation program. Gerald was upbeat and I could identify with him. Something about addicts, they can easily identify with other addicts. Gerald shared a few things about his life and the program and I started to feel better. Just maybe, I could turn this thing around. On leaving the meeting I believed life was better than death. I had survived a few days and my confidence was growing. Every now and then I would have to suppress the desire to go get high, but that was okay—at least I didn't use.

The Showers of Blessings meeting was on Tuesday. That Friday Sherry and I decided to take a ride. We managed to go a couple of safe places but it wasn't long before our addictions got hold of the wheel. We wound up among the pretty green trees of Berkley. We passed Li'l Dave, my ace, as we headed down Liberty Street. Eye contact and it was over. We stopped and he asked me to follow him. Dave offered me a half-ounce of that flaky fish-scale white cocaine. I wasted no time in accepting. I didn't take the package because I wanted to get high; I just wanted some money and this was the only way I knew. I thought I was ready. I had been locked up long enough for the drugs to be out of my system and I didn't want to get high. I was ready. I was ready all right, ready to set my foolish self up for another round of drama and danger.

I took the cocaine and cooked it into crack without using. I was running on pure willpower. Money was my focus. Any thought I had to use was beaten down by my will to make it work this time. I wanted to impress those that were still in the street. I really thought I had it. I had a half-ounce and didn't even take one toot.

I bagged up the crack and found a likely candidate to distribute the goods. Michael Ferguson was my partner in crime. Mike was loyal and I thought I could trust him to do the right thing. We made a lot of money together before and I figured this time we would do even better because I wasn't smoking. I gave Mike the package and went to Virginia Beach to wait for the results. After a couple of hours I called to check on my investment. Mike told me things were slow and he would call me when money started to come in. I called back the next hour and he gave the same report. This was a Friday—that's normally the busiest day of the week and he was claiming "things were slow." I grew concerned and headed for Berkley. When I got in the car I knew I was in trouble. My mind was racing, my heart pumping; again it was as if I had already taken a hit of cocaine. I told myself that money was the reason I was driving to Berkley, but subconsciously my addiction had taken over again.

It was a constant battle all the way to Berkley. Good and evil having a knock-down, drag-out fight in my head. By the time I reached Berkley evil had won. Mike had started smoking instead of trying to sell. I went to the house that I had left him at, and there he was, high as gas. I took the package from him. Like I could do better....I didn't have the package ten minutes before it was evident that my addiction was still the heavyweight champion of my world. There I was, struggling to put a piece of crack on the can. As they say in the programs, "One is too many and a thousand not enough." One hit turned into a night of non-stop smoking. The worst part about getting high was when all the money was gone, and there was no more dope. The feeling that you feel then was the worst for me. I hated that emptiness. Even after smoking for days that same nasty feeling would occur. We called it *fiending.*

When the package got low and I knew the money was short I made my move to find another source to supply my need. I heard Justice was on South Main Street and he had rocks. Justice was handling the package for C. I managed to talk my way into a thousand-dollar pack of crack rocks. Those too became casualties of my Friday night binge. The daylight hour was approaching and the money was short. Paying Li'l Dave was important but paying Justice weighed heavier on my mind. I'd had trouble before with Cheese, another New Yorker who was down with Justice's crew, and I didn't want another confrontation. I took off from Berkley back to Virginia Beach without a trace. I needed help fast.

When you make your mind up to do the right thing, that doesn't mean that everything will go right. In life everything may not go as planned. A friend of mine told me that "a lesson not well learned will return," so don't be so discouraged if you have to repeat a few classes. More than anything stay focused on your goal.

The problems that you have created for yourself may not disappear overnight. You took a while to get to this place. It's going to take a while to overcome your problems, but don't get down on yourself. Rome wasn't built in a day and there is no quick fix for your situation. You didn't mess it up overnight and neither will you fix it overnight. Just think about how many twists and turns it took to get to this point. So buckle up and enjoy the ride to recovery and remember to take notes because there will be a test.

NINE

Resurrection (rez' e rek' shen) *n.* 1. *the act of rising from the dead.* 2. *the state of having risen from the dead.* 3. *the bringing back of something after disuse or neglect; revival.*

So many times in my one little life I had been the victim of failure. Schools, jobs, relationships, even my attempt at being a drug dealer. Drug dealers, one of life's lowest forms of existence, yet even at that I was a miserable failure. I was not ready to give up on being clean and sober. I had no choice—if I gave up, I died. If physical death were any worse than the death I was experiencing, I wanted no part of it.

The Tuesday after my latest relapse, I was sitting in the Showers of Blessings meeting. I was afraid and disappointed. I was mostly disappointed because I let myself down. All of that "gonna drop the can" stuff was just talk and here I was again fighting for my life. I guessed it was true—once an addict always an addict. My pain poured out in the meeting. Gerald suggested that I put myself in detox. I looked around the room at the sad eyes. The saddest belonged to my mother. She had come to every meeting to support me. I could feel her pain, and I wanted to do something to change it. I decided to give detox a shot.

Detox started out great. The people there were extra nice. Later I learned that most of the staff were ex-addicts. That explains their compassion for us misfits who found ourselves in this place. They fed us three meals a day and even though being there had that jail flavor to it, this was no jail. The beds were clean and the food was good. I enjoyed being there. The meetings had substance; I started to learn about the disease that had infected me. About how this sickness didn't start just when I took my first hit of crack or my first drink. It had started long before I knew what drugs were. I learned that there was no medicine I could take and no miracle cure. This was the beginning of long road to recovery that still had a few more bumps left. One of those bumps came walking through the door.

It was Ronald, my little buddy from my get-high crew. I was thrilled to see him. I never expected him to show up here. It had been a few weeks since I had seen him. I'd always worried about Ronald. He was so young when he started selling for me and I felt somewhat responsible for him being cracked out in the street. Ronald and I enjoyed our first day together. We laughed about some of things we went through and we really started to get to know each other better. I always had a genuine love for Ronald but this two-day stay in detox made us closer. That night Ronald and I went to take the trash out. As we walked around the building, I said to Ronald, "Let's go."

Ronald was afraid of leaving detox. I explained to him, "We can't stay here forever—one day we have to leave this place. I think I'm ready."

I was feeling stronger and more aware of my disease. I wanted to test what I was feeling. I wanted to be sure. The only way I was going to be sure was to get outside the walls of that detox. Ronald and I decided to stay, but after spending three days in detox I would get my chance to see if I was ready.

I was released on Saturday morning. I don't quite remember who picked me up from the detox that morning but I do remember being afraid. I remember wondering if I really had what it took to be a regular person. I had started to feel again. I started to regain a conscience. I started to feel the pain my mother was going through having a son struggling with a crack habit. My emotions were all over the place but I believed I had what it took to make it.

I got a job the next week. A job, the very thing my fellow Airplanes and I hated most. We used to claim that if we could find the man that invented jobs, we would kill him. Now here I was, Jabba "Discount Man" Jaws, gainfully employed. I was only doing telemarketing selling light bulbs but it was good for me. I was working for the Handicap Workers of America. The deal was because I had been a drug addict I qualified to be a handicapped person. I felt guilty telling potential customers in my sells pitch "Hi, I'm Byron and I'm a handicapped person." I was leaving my old life behind and that pitch seemed a little close to deceitful.

I started to accumulate money. Not drug money, but hard-earned cash. So since *legally* I was "socially" handicapped I learned to accept the title of handicapped. The job was changing my life along with other positive activities I was doing. I hadn't turned the corner yet, but it felt like I wasn't far away. The job raised my self-esteem. I started feeling like a real man.

Showers of Blessings played a huge part in the changes that were starting to come into my life. The Showers of Blessings program was an outpatient drug support group at Bethany Baptist Church. The group would meet every Tuesday night in Pastor Jake Manley's office. This was the meeting that my mother made me agree that I would attend before she would bail me out. It proved to be a great strategy because that meeting gave me some strong tools that have helped to build a new life.

I also started to attend church services on a regular basis. During church service the Sunday after my release from detox a guy was asked to pray. I remember two things about that prayer. The first was that the guy praying had on red socks. Those socks were bright and I never will forget them. The socks were red and long on his legs. I know because during the service he got happy and started to shout. His pants were flapping and those red socks were like emergency flares. He could have flagged down planes on a deserted island with those babies. The second and more important thing was what he said while he was praying. He mentioned that he also was delivered from drugs. That caught my ear because I really wanted to be able to utter those words so I wanted to know how he was delivered. I wanted so badly to get to know the guy because he had something I wanted.

A week later a stranger showed up at a support group meeting at the church. He had heard about the group and he wanted to give a hand to help others who were struggling with drug habits. His name was Arthles Lynn, the guy who was wearing the red socks on Sunday. He shared his testimony of drug use and recovery. Big Gerald had good information but there was something different about Lynn. He was genuine.

Lynn had no problem sharing his life story with the class. His story easily caught my attention. First of all, Lynn had to be the only human on earth that had smoked as much as I did. To have smoked like that and still be alive and not locked up—he was worth listening to. Lynn was different from the others that I met in recovery. He was real and after going through a life that featured a fake father, fake friends, and fake hopes, *real* was just what I needed. He went on to tell us how long he had been clean. I never really believed that anyone was totally clean but Lynn seemed to be the closest thing to free from drugs that I had come across.

I began to trust him and I started to open up. I told him how I was trying to do everything that was being suggested to me. I was being *Honest, Open-minded* and *Willing.* I was eating the foods they told me to eat. I was going to as many meetings as I could and attending church on a regular basis, but still I had relapsed and I hated the feeling. Lynn calmly told me if I wanted to be truly free of drugs I needed to be saved. I had no idea what *saved* was. I heard about people going to church and getting saved but I didn't really know how to be saved. I remember that Greg Simon and Kung Fu back in the day confessed to be saved. They talked different for a little while but it wasn't long before they started acting the same way they were before or even worse. Nevertheless, at this point, I was willing to do whatever it took. I was just tired.

I prayed and I accepted Jesus Christ as my savior and things started to change. A lightning bolt didn't come down from the sky, I didn't fall out and wallow on the floor but something was different. I no longer felt the pressure of having to fix this mess I made by myself. I gained a new confidence about myself and I felt no one could take it away. The confidence showed in the next meeting we had at Showers of Blessings. During the meeting Big Gerald asked me how I was feeling and how I felt about my relapse. The answer I gave wasn't the answer he expected. I told him I was fine and the relapse was behind me and I thought nothing of it. He was still digging, asking more questions.

"Don't you feel any guilt or shame?"

My response was, "I'm saved now and what happened in the past doesn't make a real difference."

He had this look like I gave the wrong answer. I don't know what he was looking for but I felt I was straight. I wasn't high and I had been clean and sober for more than a week and it felt great. Something was working—maybe it was the "saved" thing. I had no desire for drugs, or even for the lifestyle.

After a couple of weeks Big Gerald stopped coming to the meetings, but Lynn became one of my best friends. I don't think Gerald really liked the way the meetings were going. Gerald was used to having a therapy-style meeting and the meeting was becoming extremely spiritual. Gerald was from a Narcotics Anonymous background and that was the way he had planned to help the people that came to Showers of Blessings. Things in the meetings started to change and the Bible became the foundation of the meeting. Gerald wound up leaving and became hard to contact. On the other hand, Lynn joined the church and became a cornerstone of the ministry. Lynn and I became close friends. I watched him closely. The relationship and the advice he gave inspired me to want to stay clean and sober.

After thirty days of being clean and sober, I was tricked by my addiction again. A thirty-day chip was given in Narcotics Anonymous meetings to signify that you had thirty days of clean time. The thirty-day chip was one of my most treasured goals. I had never made it thirty days without medicating myself with drugs or alcohol. For the first time, I finally put together thirty days of clean time, but that thirtieth day fell on Friday. Friday was a hustler's dream. Everybody who was anybody got high on Friday. I didn't want to be a fool but I couldn't help myself.

On the day when I was supposed to receive my chip, I also got the idea to try to get my hustle back on. And again, it was a Friday night, the night that I would usually make my biggest profits. There's a song that proclaims, "The freaks come out at night," and on Friday night, the freaks and the fiends would be on display. I had over four weeks clean and I had never missed so many Friday hustling nights. My whole being was crazing on this Friday. I had a choice—go to the meeting and get some more information to fight my addiction or visit Berkley and feed this somewhat smaller but still tremendously strong monkey that maintained a perch on my back. When I got in the car I knew it was monkey-feeding time. I had just gotten paid. I've never been one to get paid and go shopping or spend money on material things. I used money to make money and this Friday, that was the plan.

It wasn't long before my great idea turned into a night of misery. Even though I wanted to do the right thing my body wouldn't let me. On this particular night Sherry had given me a ride to Berkley. I ducked her once I started to get high. The car seemed to be on automatic pilot as we took off. The ride was over and Sherry and I touched down in Berkley. I wasted no time getting involved in my old behavior. I purchased a small amount of crack with the intention of selling it. I don't believe I made a dime before the purchase I made was up in smoke. Once again I was my own best customer and to make matters worse, here I was fiending. When I got that feeling nothing and nobody could keep me from my next hit. *By any means necessary* was my mindset. I had no money and no more crack. I didn't want my old associates to know that I was back in the street, so I tried to do my business on the down low. That made it hard to get enough money to support my habit. I eventually ran out of money and drugs but my craving was still intact.

Desperate for a blast, I pulled a page from Icky Boo's book and hit the corner selling soap as crack. On my first attempt it didn't work so I decided to give it a break. I settled in at one of the local crackheads' house and hoped somebody would give me a blast. I was fiending something terrible, looking out windows, walking in and out of the apartment. I needed a hit something bad.

Relief came as day began to break. Ms. Kitty, one of the more celebrated crackheads, showed up with crack. Ms. Kitty and I had met when she was with Ben, a former business associate of mine. Ben would get packages from me and go out to Oakleaf Park and make money with Ms. Kitty. Most times he smoked more than he sold. Then he'd use Ms. Kitty's money to re-up from me. He normally came alone but this day he brought Ms. Kitty with him. She walked into the house with the look of a gangster on her face. She sat down to smoke with us and after a few moments she pulled up her tee-shirt to reveal a pistol hanging around her neck by a dirty shoestring. Ben bragged that she was his assassin. After a couple of trips to my place with Kitty, Ben asked me to test her faithfulness to him. I explained to Ben this wasn't a good idea, but he insisted. It wasn't long before Ben and Ms. Kitty were no longer a couple.

On this morning, Kitty saw me in need of a fix so she helped to satisfy the craving that was eating me alive that morning. I thought that after you've been clean for a while you could go back to small amounts and it would be enough, but what I learned was that my tolerance picked up right where it left off. Kitty shared a couple of hits and then she fell asleep. She probably had been out in the street for a couple of days without sleep. I was fiending like a demon and I had to have more drugs. I managed to find her stash tucked away in a box of cigarettes. She had about seven twenty-dollar pieces of crack. I smoked them all in less than an hour. When all her crack was gone, I sat there looking like Boo Boo the fool, craving more drugs. Like the plant in "Little Shop of Horrors" my addiction was screaming "Feed me, Jabba!" and like a chicken with its head cut off I scrambled to find a way to continue this miserable adventure.

While I was sitting at the table, R.C., another dealer, entered the door. He told me that I had to go. That request set off signals in my twisted crack mind. R.C. had a habit of leaving packages in crackheads' houses. I had hit one of his stashes before. I left the house but I had every intention of returning. I squatted outside until I saw him leave. Then I immediately headed for a back window and quickly climbed through. After a few minutes of diligent searching I found my bounty. Eureka, I had hit the jackpot! It wasn't like it was a kilo or anything, but for a brother broke and fiending the ounce or more that was in the kitchen cabinet was a beautiful sight. I took everything. I escaped through the same window I entered. My heart was racing as I scurried to find a place to "beam up" or get high.

I managed to make it down the street to Ms. Kelly's house. Ms. Kelly's son was Christopher aka "Birdie" aka "Kee Kee" aka "Drop Ya Pants, Buddy" Liggions. Christopher was one of the guys that was in the little crew that sold drugs with me. Heart thumping, can in hand, I continued my binge. While I was in that back room getting high, I felt as though I could hear R.C. walking the block looking for me. With every hit I felt him drawing closer to the place where I was hiding. The paranoia overcame me and I just had to get out of that house. I gathered the rest of my drugs and made my way down the back staircase. I walked a couple of blocks to Sherry's sister's house. Sherry was there and she was angry with me but the rocks of crack I had would surely soothe her feelings of rage. As we sat there getting high there was a knock on the door.

R.C. had found me and he was accompanied by Barry Mullen and a guy known as Godfather. I hid in the closet and Sherry opened the door. They proceeded to search the house. They found me and the violence began. R.C. punched me in the mouth, leaving a scar that I carry to this day. Godfather threw in a couple of weak blows. He screamed, "Where's my stuff?" I told him I didn't have it. He said his nephew had seen me climbing out of the window of the apartment where it was stashed. I 'fessed up to keep down any future violence. I told R.C. I would deliver the package through Barry. Barry and I went way back and the scheme I was getting ready to pull would work with Barry involved. After R.C. left I took Barry back in the house and pulled a bag from under the mattress. The bag held some of the drugs I'd stolen but not all of them. The rest of the package was in a place I figured no one would look. I had hidden the rest of the drugs in the microwave oven.

Barry left and I smoked the rest of the stash and headed back to Virginia Beach. My feelings were hurt, I was broke, and I still had to deal with the fact that I never did get my thirty-day chip.

Don't be totally discouraged by minor setbacks. During your fight to conquer your negative situation you may experience a setback. Something I want to make absolutely clear: NOBODY IS PERFECT. If at first you don't succeed you know the drill—keep trying to get it done. You may be right around the corner from your deliverance. You have come too far to give up now. People have these lapses; when you have this type of setback try to figure out why. Make a note of why; if you don't physically write it down make a mental note. Especially when you know you no longer desire to be involved in these negative behaviors. Keep your head up, keep the faith, don't give up the fight.

TEN

If at first you don't succeed try, try, again. Slick little nuggets like this that I picked up in life and at the drug meeting were valuable to my recovery. Although relapse does not *have* to be a part of recovery, for me my relapses provided a great learning experience. My triggers to relapse were money, sex and my false sense of invincibility. These three things with the help of God I had to learn to overcome.

I used to think that I was invincible. I thought I was the smartest, the most charismatic; and I could overcome any obstacle without any help. I once had a discussion with my mother about how my ambition was to continue to climb the ladder of success nonstop. Everybody that got in my way would serve as the rungs beneath me. I was Superman. I was even foolish enough to believe that if I cut myself my body would heal faster than any other human being. I was high on me. I guess that was my first addiction, *me*!

I was known in high school as Byron "Slicker" Joyce, the People's Choice. This was a self-proclaimed title that gave the impression that I was a popular figure. The name was supposed to make you think of a player who was smooth with the ladies, but if truth were told I never had a relationship until I was twenty years of age. I guess that didn't qualify me as a lady-killer. I thought more of myself than I really was. People would say they thought I resembled Muhammad Ali, which only added more puff to my already enormous ego. I was the Ali of Norfolk, so fast and so pretty, I couldn't possibly be beat. I was the champ in my own mind. Don't get me wrong—there's nothing wrong with being confident, but to be overconfident can set you up for disaster. I guess Shorty, an old pool hustler who taught me a few things during my mis-education in the poolroom back in the day, probably put it best when he said I had a big head full of sawdust.

My folly kept the truth hidden from me. Truth was the real key to my freedom. The truth was that crack was a beast of an opponent and I could not overcome it without help. My addiction was still stealing points and winning rounds. He counter-punched every attempt I made to knock him out and made me look foolish again. I was engaged in real warfare against a killer opponent but quitting was not an option.

It was back to square one after this relapse. But I had learned something from this experience. I learned that at this point in my life money was not all that important because right then, money meant hustling, and hustling led to getting high, and the last thing I wanted to do was to get high. So, as I had been taught, I turned to the Power greater than myself and asked that the hustling just be taken away. For a while, I was okay. Hustling didn't really cross my mind. I went back to my little job selling light bulbs. So even though I had suffered a setback, I still had a job and most important I still had the mindset to strive to do the right thing. Even though the desire for hustling had started to subside, other problems would still arise.

I was still living in Virginia Beach. The living conditions were great. Ms. Mitchell, Sherry's adopted mother, had a nice place, a condo with two bedrooms and a loft. This was a far cry from what I was used to. The lawns were cut and trimmed. The condo had skylights in the ceiling. Ms. Mitchell and Sherry even owned a white rabbit named Valentino (Val for short). Back in the day the rabbit would have looked like a rock to me. I would have probably tried to smoke him.

Overall, I was content there but there was a tugging at my heart for Berkley. Berkley, where the crime of the century had taken place. The place where a young boy trying to discover what it was to be a man was viciously wounded and left half dead. The day came when I got that call to head back to the scene of the crime.

Whatever sacrifices that need to be made, make them. It's going to take sacrifices to obtain victory when you're trying to overcome something you have become comfortable doing. Some people are going to be disappointed with your decisions. You must keep in mind that this is about you. The life you save could very well be your own. Make no mistake about it—the people around you are important but when it come down to it you gotta do what you gotta do for you.

Get all the help you can to get success. If it takes support groups, church groups and even God himself, use it. Whatever it takes, by any means necessary get the job done.

ELEVEN

There was a slogan on the street that went, "Visitors make prisoners." This phrase was used as an excuse for not visiting when someone had gotten locked up. The saying is kind of true. A visit back to Berkley would be the reason you could almost call me a prisoner of Berkley today. The place I didn't want to go as a young, scared teenager had somehow become home.

I was still addicted to Berkley, so every now and then I would slip in and slip out just to get my fix of the Berkley air. I couldn't stay long because there was still a little matter of a thousand-dollar debt that hadn't been paid. The bill was with those crazy New York boys and I didn't have any money to pay. Once I ran into Bernard "Pee Wee" Thompson. Pee Wee was a guy who had worked at the Berkley Community Center. Pee Wee would pick me up when I was on drugs and ride me around and just talk. His talks would give me hope that one day I could recover from the sickness I was experiencing. During this particular trip to Berkley, Pee Wee told me he missed me and asked me how I was doing. I told him I was doing well. I also let him know that I had been clean and sober for a couple of months and that I was staying in the Beach.

Pee Wee suggested that I consider moving back to Berkley. He believed that God was cleaning me up for a reason, and wanted to use me. Now, I had not been back in the church that long. I say "back" because when I was nineteen, maybe twenty, my mother made an effort to get me in church. I went for a while, but I drifted back out again. The only thing I really remember was smoking one of the biggest jays ever the day before my baptism, vowing not to do it any more. Within a two-week period I was smoking again. Anyhow, this idea of God using me was just crazy. What in the name of rolling paper did God want to do with me? Had he run out of qualified people? I always knew Pee Wee was strange but this had to be an all-time highlight from his strangest moments file. I paid it no mind and went about my business.

But a week later that same idea came back to mind. I had been clean and sober about three months now. I was going to Showers of Blessings regularly and I felt stronger than ever. I was a devoted member of the church. Things had started to look great for me. One day that inner voice spoke and asked, *Why not go back?*

I felt it was the Lord speaking. I said, "If I go back them New York boys gonna kill me."

The voice answered, *If you go back I'll go with you.*

For me to be clean for over three months there had to be something else at work. Though I was afraid, I trusted that voice.

Sherry was still dabbling in drugs and I felt I needed to get away from her. During that week I came in from work and she pulled out a big rock of cocaine. She claimed that she found it in my pocket and suggested maybe it was left over from my last binge. I grabbed the rock and dropped it in the toilet. It took all I had in me and more, but I pushed the handle to flush the poison down. With every circle it made going down I wanted to reach in and grab it but I let it go and was happy I did. The fact that I could do such a task made me start to feel more confident that my deliverance was on the way. But I was still living with Sherry and Sherry still wanted to get high. I can't prove it, but I believe she bought crack just so I'd get high with her. The meetings taught us to change our usual people, places, and things. Sherry was the person, Ms. Mitchell's condo was the place, and getting high was the thing. I wasn't going to let Sherry or any other creature stop my progress.

That Sunday morning I told Sherry and Ms. Mitchell I had to go. It was very emotional. By then Sherry had lost the twins and I no longer felt obligated to her. Ms. Mitchell and I cried all the way to church. Sherry didn't go because she was out until the wee hours the night before. I cried because I knew I was leaving a phase of my life behind, but more than that I cried out of fear of the fate that lay ahead for me in Berkley.

The first couple of weeks I spent in seclusion. I stayed in the house; I only left to go to church and work. I knew the boys were still in business on the other end of South Main and I wanted no part of a confrontation. After that first couple of weeks I started to venture out. I would take a walk in the neighborhood but only through the back streets. The back street strategy paid off for a while until one day I stretched my boundaries too far. While I was walking down Indian River Road a car passed by. The car stopped at the corner. Five fellows popped out of the car and I knew them well. Job in the Bible said it best—"The thing that I feared most has come upon me." Those New York guys finally had their chance to spot me. My first instinct was to cut and run but I figured that could get ugly, so I just stood there. The most flamboyant of the group, one spoke first.

"Jaws, where that money at, bro?"

My answer was short and with all humility I said, "Man, I'm saved now and I don't know how I'm going to get that money."

The response I got surely wasn't what I expected. They all kind of looked at each other, looked at me and started laughing. Then they got in their car and drove away.

There's a saying that I first heard from Chico. The saying is "Word is bond." What it means is that you need to abide by your words if you are to be respected. I guess the voice I'd heard, the voice that told me that he would go with me if I returned to Berkley, was true to his word. A couple of weeks after that incident I became bolder. I started to walk on the front streets. While on a trip to the store one day I saw C, the leader of the New York boys. I didn't know how he would receive me but after a few moments I saw his smile. I walked up and gave him a handshake. He asked me how I was. I answered that I was okay but I could use something to eat. He reached in his pocket and gave me twenty bucks and instructed me to stay safe. I walked away in amazement.

Even though I came out well from that situation, my addiction was still lurking and it would get the chance to make me look foolish again. I had been back at 1002 South Main Street maybe thirty days and was celebrating ninety days clean time. During my time on the streets, I had bought the house and given it to my mom because my addiction got so bad I couldn't afford to stay there. I had become one of the favorites in the Showers of Blessings meetings and on the program's radio show. People were inspired by the fact that a wretch like me was clean and sober and it seemed I would be that way forever. Crack addicts and heroin users started coming to the church to see what Showers of Blessings had done for Byron Joyce. The addicts believed if I could do it, anybody could. I had started walking in the same streets where I used to deal, telling people how well I was doing. The guys that use to sell for me wanted to hang around me. Things were going well until I dropped my guard and was hit with a sucker punch.

I had hooked up with Pee Wee. Pee Wee was selling hats, really nice hats. I saw an opportunity to make some money. I should have been wary of this setup, knowing that money was a trigger for me, but I wasn't. I persuaded Pee Wee to give me the hats to sell. He knew I could make the money; I was the best there ever was. I could sell perfume to a skunk. Pee Wee didn't hesitate to give me the hats. By nightfall I had sold most of them. I made good money for Pee Wee and a nice piece of change for myself. Pee Wee paid me and offered me a ride home. I refused the ride because my addiction had already kicked in and I had other plans.

I walked from his house straight to Stafford Street. This time I really wasn't looking to get high but I wanted some of that crazy sex I was used to in the street. I searched for a while and ran into a young lady who was close to me. I used to run my operation out of her house. I was comfortable with her and this would be the perfect hit. I gave her money to go score. Because of the respect I had for her I didn't want her to feel like a hooker. She returned with the drugs and she started to smoke. She blew the smoke in my face and away I went. We smoked the rest of the crack and I never even thought about the sex again.

I stayed out all night until about five in the morning. I went home, sat down on the porch and began to cry. While I was crying I thought about all the people that would be touched by this blunder. I thought about how hard it would be to face the people at Showers of Blessings. I thought about my mom and how she'd be hurt by this episode. In hindsight, I guess my thinking about people who'd be hurt was a good thing. Before, it didn't matter who knew or who would be affected. I've smoked a can walking down the middle of the street with no concern at all, but now things were different.

Around six o'clock my mother came out the front door. I sat there on the porch with my head down. I was feeling so low. When that door opened I felt lower. She already knew what had happened. She never raised her voice or got ugly at all.

She just said, "Well, you messed up. All you can do is get up and try again." Those few words helped me a lot. It made me feel as though she believed in me and she was with me all the way.

She said "Go get some rest and you'll feel better."

This was a surprise for me. My mother was the disciplinarian of the family. Though I was too old to be getting beatings I thought she would at least say something sharp and hurtful. I got up from the porch feeling I still could do this.

It wasn't really a surprise that I was high. I kind of set myself up. At the meetings they taught us about people, places, and things and how to stay away from negative ones, yet I saw trouble and just kept going. I thought maybe because I was selling a legal product—hats—that it wouldn't affect me, but I was wrong. Hustling was hustling. And the hustling set me up to think that the sex was a safe situation for me and it wasn't. Another relapse, but again, another lesson.

People found out quickly that I had relapsed. Early that morning, while I was trying to sleep off the night before, the phone started ringing. It was as though I was being watched on closed circuit television. Everybody was calling for the scoop. My answer to each one of the calls was the same. "I know why I relapsed," I told them. The honesty that I was developing helped. I was honest enough to tell them that I wanted some sex and the sex led me to the drugs. They were in awe that I'd admit such a thing. *He was in the church, why did he still want sex?*

But they knew that they had the same desires. I refused to lie. I wanted to be real. That realness has stayed with me to this day. I wasn't out to impress people, it was God I was trying to impress. God was the one who had the power to free me, so nobody else's opinion really counted. I felt God understood anyway and if I really asked he would deliver. He did it with the New York boys situation. The people that came around to my house expected me to look defeated but I still believed I had a shot to make it.

I started my journey again with more zeal than before. I rushed to get back to the next Showers of Blessings meeting. I was one of the first to get out of my seat to talk. Although a lot of the people in the meeting looked up to me, I had to tell about my fall the day before. It was like a weight was lifted from my shoulders when I confessed my blunder.

Many people at the meeting embraced me and wished me well. I started going to every church service I could find. On Fridays I would go from church to church until I couldn't find one open. I wanted this clean and sober thing and I would fight any challenge to get it done. But it wouldn't be long before my next challenge would come.

March 24, 1991 was my next bump in the road. Hustling didn't set up this day of relapse. Again, lust was the cause of my fall. I was in the church and I didn't want to get involved with a churchwoman. I felt that churchgoing women were so holy that casual sex couldn't happen with them. (Boy, was I wrong, but that's another book!) I went out that night strictly to experience the high of getting laid or something close. I had no money so I made my way to my brother Doo-Wop. I found him in Priscilla's house. I told him I wanted to trick and asked if he could help me. He gave me a piece of rock cocaine.

I found my victim and headed for the back room. This time I'd be smarter. I told the girl, "You can't use this in front of me. Let's finish and then you can get high."

She pleaded to let her smoke first. I knew if she got high in front of me, I might follow the same pattern as before. I wanted her so bad that her arguments started to sound good. She said "Once I get high you know I'm *really* gonna get into you."

I agreed and the rest was history. It seemed as though things were moving in slow motion. She placed burnt ashes on the can after she carefully poked a hole in it. Gently, she placed the small piece of white crack on the bed of ashes. The flick of the lighter was as if she was starting a forest fire. She placed her lips on the mouth of the can and inhaled. My body cringed to the sound of her sucking the smoke out of that can. She set the can down and the smoke danced out the mouth of the can and across the small table. It looked like a rock show as the smoke appeared to cover the table like smoke covers the stage at a concert. Within seconds I grabbed the can and jammed it to my face.

I was high again. I sat there for a few minutes feeling stupid, and then I went to my brother to get some more crack. He opened the door, looked in my eyes and said, "Oh, lord."

He could see the stupid crackhead look in my face. At first I felt too proud to ask for some more crack, but my pride quickly disappeared and I asked for another piece. He gave me one and told me, "That's all you gonna get. You need to go home."

I went back, smoked what was left, and went out into the hallway of the apartment. After standing there for a short while I noticed another guy. I asked him, "Do I look more stupid than anybody else out here?"

His answer was "Yep."

Since he was high as a kite and his eyes looked like a deer's in headlights, if I really looked stupider than *he* did, it was time to leave. I didn't hesitate and went straight home.

It all came together that next day as I sat and thought about the night before. I didn't write out a list, but if I did it would look like this:

- If I sell drugs most likely I'll use them.
- Hustling for money has led me to drug use.
- Associating with people who use crack has led to drug use.
- Hustling and sex are strong triggers of my crack addiction.
- There will be negative consequences from my drug use.
- Confidence is good but overconfidence can be dangerous.
- One is too many and a thousand is not enough.
- The worst feeling I have ever felt in my life is fiending for drugs.

Equipped with this information I was set to make life better for myself. This life would later prove to be profitable for both me and my community.

There will be no magic potion, nor a strike of lightning from heaven that is going to change your situation. If you really want to make a difference in your life you must first figure out why. Why do I want to change? Why do I do what I do? Why are the triggers that cause me to return to the same negative behaviors so effective?

Don't trust the information you come up with to memory. It was so revealing to me as I prepared this book that the bullets list I put together helped to make my recovery so real. Just looking at the list helped me to see my addiction was powerful. It also assisted me with the fact that my addiction was related to a lot of different things in my life. When compiling this list be honest with yourself. Don't try to sugar-coat it; be as raw as you need to be to get the message across to yourself that this is a terrible time in your life. Make it known that some people don't survive where you are. Your list of truth (as I call it) will be your road map to a successful recovery.

Another thing to remember is you can't do this by yourself. Your situation is not unique. I read somewhere that "there is nothing new under the sun." Trust me; you are not the only one who has done what got you in trouble. There are countless numbers of individuals who are also experiencing what is causing your collapse. Not only that, there are a lot of people who have been where you are and made it out. Seek those who are trying to get out of what you are stuck in, whatever the case. Your fellowship should be with those who have been set free from what you have been through.

TWELVE

Life (lif) *n* 1. *The period between birth and death.* I've been clean and sober now some seventeen years. A lot of people thought I wouldn't ever make it. As the great Hotdog (a fellow Airplane) would say "I've been around the world once and seen it twice." I've seen people reclaim their lives from the grip of death. I've seen others walk the dangerous white line until it took everything they owned, their freedom and their lives.

For me, the high wasn't worth the consequences. I often say that if I could be sure that I didn't have to suffer the negative effects of the drug, I would get high right now. It wasn't that I didn't like the feeling and taste of the drug but I hated the side effects.

I became deeply involved in the church. For over ten years I was the regular spokesperson on the Showers of Blessings radio broadcast. This broadcast was launched to show drug addicts and alcoholics that they could get their lives on track through the program. Hundreds of addicts have made their way to Showers of Blessings and gotten their lives back together. For some their lives got even better than they were before they started drugs.

Donnie "Icky Boo" Mann followed me into the program after he was brutally beaten in the street. You remember Icky Boo—he was the guy who couldn't sell enough dummy cocaine. But he'd eventually get his fill of playing tricks on people. The young dealers warned Donnie not to sell dummies on the block. These young guys were different from the old school boys such as myself. They were the offspring of the crack addicts who were still in the street. These jokers were angry and didn't care who knew it. They found out that Donnie was still running the scam even after their warning, so they punished him. Donnie was beaten badly at the hands of these young men.

When I heard the news about Donnie's beating I rushed to remove him from the house where they left him. When I entered the house, I was afraid that I had gotten there too late. The house was abandoned. It was dark and musty. I entered hesitantly and hollered for Donnie. I didn't get a response so I called for him again. After some silence I heard a very faint voice. I listened closely and I heard a whimper. I moved toward the sound and found Donnie in a back room. He looked one hot mess. It was hard to believe this was a guy I looked up to as a teenager, a neighborhood icon who had been reduced to a beaten, smelly, crackhead.

I took Donnie to my house and called for help. I called my best friend Mike, a local news reporter who had befriended me at the Showers of Blessings program. Mike asked me to keep Donnie for the night. When morning came Mike took Donnie to his house. Later, he made arrangements for Donnie to attend a rehab in Pennsylvania. It's good to know that Donnie is still going strong to this day. Others weren't so lucky.

Ronald was one of the unlucky ones. When I left the street I kept tabs on Ronald. He was still doing his thing in the street. After a while, Ronald went into the Job Corps, where he earned a rep as a knockout artist. It was hard to believe that this skinny frail kid had developed into a noted street fighter, but that was the case. After his return from the Job Corps Ronald showed up at my house. We talked about old times and had a few laughs. He even told me about some of the skirmishes he was involved in and how he was knocking people out. I let him know that people in this day and age wouldn't keep taking the butt whippings that he was serving; one of these people might retaliate.

One morning I went jogging with Ronald and told him that maybe we could turn his golden punch into a career as a boxer. He admitted that he might want to try the boxing thing. That was the last time I saw him alive.

I heard Ronald had gotten into a fight with some guys and beat a couple of them down. Later Ronald was ambushed in Huntersville and killed. I felt as if I had lost a family member. I had to leave his funeral early to compose myself. I'll always remember the pain I felt sitting there helpless. He was dead. What was left for me to do? *Another one bites the dust...que sera, sera...*and any other worthless saying that fit my pitiful plight. *Maybe I'm still high and this is just a bad trip I'm on and when I come down everything will be all right.*

I was clean and sober, but I was learning that life was no joke. Maybe that's the reason I stayed high for so long. Maybe I was trying to escape reality. But here it was smack dab in my face. I was a black man in America and my life and the lives of others like me didn't matter at all to some folk. Reality was, the fathers of children like me had been tricked into not caring about the welfare of their children or families and had left them in this wilderness to fend for themselves. Reality was, there were thousands of little Byron Joyces all over these United States hoping their daddies would show up and take their rightful places in their sons' lives. Reality was, if things were really going to change for me I had to transform my thinking to take my life to the next level. And while I was at it, I had to transform the lives of others, too.

My transformation was coming along well and opportunities for me to help others would soon come.. By now I was married and unemployed, and my family was surviving on food stamps, Medicaid and Section 8 housing. Though as a young man I swore off jobs, I was ready to change my vow. I had been making some money selling tee shirts and things on the street but the demand was greater than the resource. I was officially ready to get a job.

No doubt my life had changed, married and now considering a job—there is a God. In my search for employment I was told about a possible opening at a local Boys and Girls Club in the Campostella area of Norfolk. I knew this area well; a lot of my time was spent there trying to score drugs. Ironically, a drug elimination grant was being used to hire people like me. When I say like me, I mean a person with a checkered past and a criminal record. I was a convicted felon with a history of drug abuse and I was applying for a position to work with children. What was I thinking? This doesn't make sense to a crazy person. Me, Byron Joyce aka Jabba aka Discount Man, the former king of crack, trying to work for one of the leading youth development organizations in the country? Fat chance. Once again my conventional wisdom failed me and I was hired. But now what?

This job would prove to be destiny. The pay was barely minimum wage but I was just crazy about the fact that I had a legitimate job. I went in and worked hard. It wasn't long before I became the most popular staff member in the building with the youth. They all started to flock around me. I became known as Mr. B. At first it was just a job, but it wasn't long before my feeling about this would change. The children for the most part only wanted to come to my area. I started out in the gamesroom, they stayed in the gamesroom. When I was moved to the gym as the athletic director the gym became the hangout. The promise of gifts from other staff could only tear them away for a little while. Those children loved Mr. B and I loved them, too. My relationship with the children continued to grow and so did my popularity in the whole Campostella community.

I still needed money for my family and the minimum wage just wasn't cutting it for me financially, so at the request of a friend I put in an application with the Virginia Employment Commission for a position at the Ford plant. It wasn't long before I was interviewed and I got the job. Ford was paying big bucks so I was happy to hear the news. I started to share my good news with everyone and for the most part people were happy for me. My feelings changed when one of the children made a statement. His words cut to the core of my very being.

He said, "You just like the rest of them. Get a better job and just leave us."

I took the job at Ford but the words of that young man never left my spirit. I felt as though I had left my life behind. Every night I left the Ford plant I wondered what was happening with those children. The money was good at Ford but it was just a job. A cold, impersonal, non-inspirational job. Every night I left the plant I prayed for God to deliver me from that job. My heart longed to be with the kids at the club. I was eventually released from the plant for my complaint about my knee. I had some pain from my knee but my major pain was my absence from Campostella Boys and Girls Club. After being released I returned to the club to the happy faces of the children I had left.

These were children like I used to be. I knew that these children, though I could make them smile for a little while, were under attack. If a city is not well guarded it will eventually fall prey to attackers that come to overtake it, steal its spoils and leave it desolate. So many young lives in inner city neighborhoods have been raped and pillaged and I guess God had anointed me protector of these valuable cities. The Oakleaf and Diggs areas had households primarily run by women. Only three percent of the children that came to my Boys and Girls club had both a mother and father in the house. Some of those fathers were stepfathers or just a live-in boyfriend. The area was known for drug dealing and drug abuse. High criminal activity was a result of the impoverished conditions in this area. The expectation for children of this area was that they would grow up and repeat the same mistakes as their families. The very same expectations that society had also placed on me. I was determined to make a change. Maybe this was my way of making up for all the destruction I had done in the past. It was my mission to change lives. I no longer had a problem with drugs and alcohol so life was pleasant for me. I had time to dedicate to these children. The Boys & Girls Club was the vehicle I would use to fulfill my calling. Whatever they wanted I tried to supply—music, trips, prizes, and especially sports.

    I would get an opportunity to play a bigger role in the Boys and Girls Club. Upon my return to the club I learned that my supervisor had applied for and received another job. His departure left a vacancy in the unit director position. On paper I wasn't even a candidate for the position. I only had a GED education and the position required completion of four years of college. I had worked every position in the club and had knowledge of the whole operation. I knew it was a tough sale, but hey, I had no business even working there so I figured what can I lose. I approached those in charge of hiring personnel. They provided their excuses why they couldn't hire me but I was persistent with the reasons why they should. In the end my persistence paid off. They gave me the job. Byron C. Joyce, the new Unit Director of the Campostella Boys and Girls Club.

    I was on a mission. I knew I was expected to fail so I determined to prove everyone wrong. I had developed such a strong bond with the kids that moving to the new position would come easy. I developed a strong staff and then put out the programs that would be used to change the lives of the young people at the club. Before I came to the club I volunteered as a basketball coach in Berkley. I spent a lot of time developing a basketball program at the club. The season was successful and the relationships that were born through that team were tight. I decided to use basketball as the foundation of the club. So added to my responsibility to run the facility was basketball coach.

The relationships that came from basketball developed a new branch to my family tree. A couple of players from my team at Berkley came up to Campostella to play with me. Terrance Mayo and Bryan Perrin were the players. Terrance was the son of a young lady with a drug problem. Not only did he play ball but he loved just hanging around me. Most weekends Terrance stayed at my house. Our relationship started to grow. Eventually Terrance's mother offered me custody of him. I was happy to take him into my home. I was just happy to give him a better place to live and grow up. I was just happy to provide that wall of protection to help deter the some of the attacks on his city.

Bryan was a big twelve year old when I met him. I had to pay him to come to practice. He looked forward to that dollar I would pay him. After he learned the game I no longer had to pay for his services. As these young people started to be placed in my life I began to realize why I was still around. I guess that's why those shots aimed at me didn't connect, and why, when I could have gotten serious time for the crimes I committed, I was released or received light sentences. Looking back I can see that this was my calling, this was my mission, touching the lives and being a support system to young people. Terrance and Bryan became like family. They even begin to call me "Pop."

Basketball served as the main draw. We put together five teams at the club and entered them in the City of Norfolk Parks and Recreation league. Normally, Boys and Girls Clubs teams were not good enough to compete in the city league. Our teams competed and were some of the best teams in the league. I coached three out of the five teams. I was sometimes late coming to games because I was coaching another team across town. When I showed up you could tell the difference in the kids. They would pep right up when I walked in the gym. The other teams knew they were in trouble. These young men would just respond to me. There was something about our relationship that would make them try anything I asked. I can recall one situation when I asked them to wear soccer uniforms to start the playoffs. The uniforms were short, tight, and purple. These guys wore those uniforms with no hesitation. They fought hard throughout the playoffs and lost in the semi-final game to the team that would eventually win the city championship.

The number of youth coming to the club grew tremendously. Our attendance at the club grew from the time I became unit director. We went from an attendance of sixty-five children per day to well over a hundred. The children would love to stay at the club. At night you had to put them out. The following basketball season we expanded to nine basketball teams.

Two of the nine teams were girls' teams. Popularity of the program began to spread not only in the neighborhood but throughout the city. We started to win city championships and most of all the attitudes and behaviors of the children at the club started to change. Parents heard what was happening at the club and called by the drove to see if there was something I could do with their sons and daughters. Every day one of the children would claim me as a father. I guess they figured if Brian and Terrance could claim me as "Pop" they could, too.

I had gone from the role of being a mentor and coach to being a surrogate parent. I spent most of my time with these children. At the club, cutting their hair, taking them to eat, buying them necessities, and even delivering food to their houses—whatever it took I was willing to do.

One guy in particular that comes to mind was Russell Branch. Russell came from Youngs Park across the bridge in downtown Norfolk not far from where I grew up in Tidewater Park. Russell was quiet, reserved, but he could really play basketball. One summer I convinced him to play with me in the Berkley Summer League down in Berkley. He agreed. He always carried a backpack on his back; I figured it was just gym clothes since he was a ball player. Years later I found out that when we met Russell was selling marijuana and the book bag was his stash. Russell was such a good player I knew he could play high school ball and even college. I inquired about his grades; he quickly answered they were fine. After investigating the matter I found out that Russell barely went to school and couldn't read too well. I approached his mother to be listed on his school records so I could check on him. She was happy to do it. She was having problems of her own and I was a welcome blessing to take care of her son. I went to parent-teacher conferences, delivered food to his house, and even went to get him out of bed in the morning for school if I had to. Once in a conference with his math teacher, the teacher was telling me that Russell was not performing well in his class. I asked the teacher to put one of the algebra problems on the board. I had never taken algebra before but I had heard of the "Please Excuse My Dear Aunt Sally" rule. I used the rule and what math skills I had to work the problem on the board. Russell figured I'd never get it right. After the completion of the problem the teacher acknowledged that I was absolutely correct. Russell just looked on in disbelief but it changed something in him. I never heard of another problem he had in math or any other subject in high school.

Russell responded beautifully. He worked hard enough to bring his grades up to make him eligible to play high school ball at Booker T. Washington High School for the second half of the season. His grades continued to climb and most of his entire attitude toward the right things in life started to change. He started to stay with me on weekends and during the summers. I was his "Pops" and all of my children, even the extended ones, became his brothers and sisters. Russell later attended Redemption Christian Academy. Russell parlayed his basketball into a college scholarship to Voorhees College in South Carolina where he received his bachelor's degree and later attended Troy University where he earned his Master's degree.

After we had used basketball to get the children in the clubs, education became our main staple to elevate the children's' lives, the club and the community. Not only were we winning basketball games but the youth of the club started to achieve academic excellence. The Youth of the Year award is the highest honor given to a youth in the Boys & Girls Clubs of America. The award was won two years back to back for the Hampton Area by youths from the Campostella Boys & Girls Club. Nakia Madison won it the first year and Nicanor Williams the next. Nicanor, or Nick as we commonly call him, went on to capture the Youth of the Year title for the whole state of Virginia and the Washington, D.C. area. He and I were flown out to Chicago where he appeared on the Oprah Winfrey Show. While on Oprah he received a twenty-five thousand dollar scholarship to go to college. Nick trusted me as a father figure and to this day I am the closest thing to a father he knows. The benefits of seeing these guys and girls mature and live a productive life are more than enough compensation for the little part I played in their lives. Nick went to school for a while and then enlisted in the Army and served in Iraq. Nakia went on to acquire her Master's Degree.

Some of the youths found trouble before they found their way back to me. Edward "Keon" Mitchell was one of my sons that kind of drifted away and found his way back. I read somewhere that "If you train up children in the way they should go, when they becomes old they won't depart from that training." Keon made his way back to the club after dropping out of school. He used to be one of my top basketball players but strayed away and didn't do the things he needed to do to be successful. By now he was a father and was introduced to the drug game. One day he stumbled back to the club and you could see in his eyes he wasn't happy with his situation. After talking to him a while I offered him a job. I told him if he went and got his high school diploma I would give him a dollar raise. He obtained his GED in a few months. Today Keon is one of the top workers in the Wal-Mart system and he is completing his bachelor's degree at Norfolk State University. He is one of my closest sons and his son calls me grandpa. Keon's trouble led him back to someone he trusted and I'm so glad I was there to do what I have been accustomed to do.

So many lives were changed by God allowing my life to go on. The changes in my life had nothing to do with me but everything to do with the people I would come in contact with. Young people who society said had no chance to escape their desperate situations, now have become positive, productive, citizens because of the influence I had in their lives. People like Tiara Simmons who came out to the club a wild thirteen year old who trusted me enough to try basketball when she knew nothing about the game. Tee-Tee, as we called her, was so funny. She was the smallest thing in the club but if you let her tell it she was the baddest. Our biggest dilemma was when I told her she was going to be the point guard for the team. She did not want to try to handle that ball. After a couple of weeks I convinced her to try and she did well. That was just my way of giving her confidence to try new things. She hung around the club like it was her second home. She grew from a skinny little girl with a loud mouth who statistics say would wind up pregnant, to a young lady who attends her local church and has graduated from Norfolk State University with her bachelor's degree. She now takes time to help out other young girls who had become mothers at a young age. Tiara calls the girls her "baby mommas." Tiara has grown to be a strong young lady and it makes me feel so good to know that she is truly my daughter. She's a positive statistic and she's stable and prepared to create change everywhere she goes. Tiara was just another example of why that miserable life I had was allowed to go on just a little while longer.

When I'm asked how many children I have, I answer with all honesty *hundreds*, because I feel like every one of the children God has placed in my life is mine. They feel the same and they all call me Pop or Dad. And just think—I could have died out there. One of the bullets fired by Cheese could have hit me instead of the car. I smoked so much crack my heart could have busted in my chest, but He had another plan. You know, looking back, I never was a bad person. I had bad guidance and made bad decisions. I can't really blame anyone for my life; neither does any man get the credit for my recovery. I've always had high expectations for myself, but I never really experienced life until I started to learn what my purpose was. I used to question my existence. Why was I here? No one can truly say that they know why they were sent here, but in the years since I've been clean and sober, I'm starting to feel I'm right where I'm supposed to be. I don't regret the life I've led because it made me the man I am. I had set up a kingdom and had a fool for a king. Thank God it was overthrown and that king was left for dead. Overcoming obstacles in life can come with a great degree of difficulty but it can be done. At one time I thought that I would never make it, but today I'm free with no desire to return to that same foolishness. I was lost, but now I'm found, was blind but now I see. Half dead only means that you're still half-alive.

Praise for Half-Dead

Half-Dead is a great testimonial! Honest and forthcoming, it's inspiring and packed with practical advice. If one decides to adhere to the counsel provided in this text positive change will certainly follow.

—*Maurice Moore*

I read Mr. Byron Joyce's book *Half-Dead* the day I received it. Once I cracked it open, I could not put it down. The book puts you in the driver's seat of a journey through life—growing up, jail, poverty, despair, gangster life, drugs and personal sacrifices.... It's a must-read in today's society, and a self-motivator for anyone! It gave me a new perspective on the way I conduct my business as a Police Officer, and how I look at people. I see them in a whole new light, and now consider their upbringings in the way I treat people and react to certain situations. This book was helpful to me in many different ways, and especially helpful in knowing that [Bryon] was able to go through all this and still be a role model and sucessful to this day. If I had to put it in one word, Mr. Joyce's book is RIVETING. I read it, cover to cover, in three and a half hours.... He has a will to survive and a heart of a lion. Nothing would bring Mr. Joyce to rock bottom; he believed in himself too much, and cared about others way too much. He has a will to survive. I will read this book again, there is no doubt. I also enjoyed the numerous funny little stories; they kept me smiling throughout the book. Congratulations on a job well done, and I hope to read a sequel..... I am sure there are many lives that have been changed through his works, and would like to know about them also.

—*Officer Jeff Whitson, Portsmouth Police Dept.*

Mr. Byron C. Joyce is an experienced and acclaimed motivational speaker. To arrange an appearance, please email Byron at

jabba19_2000@yahoo.com

www.byronjoyce.com

For information on quantity discounts or fundraising with Half-Dead, call Avventura Press at 570-876-5817 or email lee@avventurapress.com

www.avventurapress.com

Order HALF-DEAD at www.avventurapress.com or by calling 570-876-5817, or fax your credit card number and expiration date to 570-876-6758.

You can also order by mail from Avventura Press, 133 Handley St., Eynon PA 18403. Please enclose your check or money order for $16 (includes priority shipping).